AUTH

Let me say first, I a… grandparents. Each one of them provided me with the basics I needed to live a good life. But often, I didn't know that when it was happening. My mother and dad's goal was to get out of impoverished West Virginia and lead a better life. I benefited tremendously with their success, but as the yiddish saying goes, **"Man makes plans and God laughs."**

I'm going to share with you the story of my early life, along with thoughts of what was in my mind at the time, from the very beginning that took me through elementary, high school, and college in the 1940's, '50's and early '60's. I'm doing this, because I thought it was a very strange way to grow up, but since I've written about it in my first book West Virginia in the Rear View Mirror, people have come to me and told me their life was similar. But it's still an unusual life. I'll also tell you a tiny bit about what was going on in the world in those days.

At the same time, pay attention to the story of my mother, Gatha Gae Ramsey Roberts, who I was at odds with for most of my early childhood. I only lived with her and my father for six years. I was never close to them when I was growing up, but as I got older I began to especially see the problems my Mother faced. Before she died, she and I spent thirty years of closeness that we had never enjoyed before. We both had been through the wash more than once, sometimes the same wash.

As you read our stories, recognize the **Yin and Yang** in our lives. Yin represents qualities including darkness, femininity, and receptivity. Yang is composed of light, masculinity, and activity. Together they provide balance and harmony in nature. That's all I'm going to say about **Yin and Yang**, but I want you to see the balanced and the unbalanced in our lives, and use that knowledge in your life.

Conventional wisdom tells us that at any given time, we are the sum of the experiences we've had through life to this point. I believe that. I am what I've experienced in my life. I hope you will identify with several of them, and consider the lessons from the others. I talk a lot about my life in school. I concentrate on this, because it is an important part of any young person's life. I hear from my children who are involved in education that things are totally different today. I feel my story provides a look into life after WWII, different from most people's but the same, too. Older citizens will remember what I talk about, so this story is for the young and the old, so enjoy a look-see into the '40's,'50's and '60's from my eyes.

I write for two reasons. One, to show young people about life back then, so they will have a base to learn and get information about what was going on back then. The second reason is to entertain older people who can say, "I remember that." The stories are true. I changed some names and things to protect people who might be upset if I talked about their relatives. Like life, some of the stories are sad, some are humorous. Some are neither, but I'll tell them to you anyway. So, young or old, if you don't know a word, a phrase or a name, Google 'em. It's fun. If someone or something from the past interests you, use Wikipedia. It's awesome.

The Leander and Ramsey post offices are gone now, but you can still find Ramsey and Leander on Google maps, reasonably close to Ansted. Follow the Saturday Road (Rt 3) from Rt 60 at Victor until you come to where the

Saturday Road meets the Sunday Road. The road over the ridge has been rerouted to a shortcut that Grandad and I used to walk before there was even a path. I'm not kidding about the names of the roads. The legend is that a long time ago, on a Saturday, a man rode a horse from the Midland Trail, (Rt 60) at Victor, into the wilderness and spent the night near the Gauley River. The next day, Sunday, he rode out to the Midland Trail at Hico. Now, from Hico it's only a short distance to the New River Gorge Bridge. Mother and I lived near the intersection of the two roads, but not at the same time, at least not for very long, but we used the Saturday Road.

Before I start to tell you about how I grew up, I'd like to thank everyone. First, thanks to Mother and Dad and my Grandparents. My grandparents gave me the basic understanding of right and wrong and taught me about a gazillion things. Mother and Dad gave me another gazillion things in different areas. A special thanks to Jim, and Jan, my brother and sister who helped me through the years. As I was the oldest, from the beginning I used them to learn how to interact with children. I was a child too, and Mother used me to watch them and care for them, and they put up with that as I learned somewhat roughly, about how to be a parent. They also inspired me, helped me write this story, and followed me throughout its life. Thanks, you two. Thanks to my very successful children, Rick, Jay, Patrick, and Becca. They have been an inspiration to me and have always supported me. We are separated in distance somewhat, but close in spirit.

Thanks to Mimi Grimes, my bridge partner, and supporter, who helped get this written, and gave me the title for this story. Thanks to my Beta Readers, Vernell Doyle, Kathleen Wettengel, Pam Henry, and Linda Wolfersheim. I also thank the hundreds of people I met and worked with throughout my life. Yes, I literally worked with hundreds of people, but that's another story. The story I'm telling you now is about how I grew up to be able to work with industry leaders, and move beyond selling and carrying gallons of buttermilk up hundreds of steps, although doing that is important work too. I'm glad that people still do it.

Now sit down, and pay attention.

Part One

Life in West Virginia

Mother And Mom

I was afraid of my mother, so I really didn't want to go with her when she borrowed Grandad's '38 Chevy pickup to go visit her sister Sybil. I was probably three years old but I remember that trip. At Sybil's, I was lying on her carpet with my eyes closed when Sybil turned her big old Hoover carpet cleaner on close to me. Startled, I opened my eyes to see that Hoover headlight staring at me. It marked me for life. When Mother drove back to Grandad's, at her insistence, I put my head on her right leg to take the nap that I'd missed at Sybils. Mother was moving her leg up and down as she braked, accelerated, and shifted gears in the pickup, navigating the ups. downs and turns on the mountains of the Saturday Road. I didn't like being around Mother in the first place, so all in all, It was not much of a nap.

I was born on October 1,1939, exactly one month after Hitler invaded Poland. My mother, Gatha Ramsey Roberts, left me with her parents in Leander, WV. on November 15th, only 45 days later, and went to live in DC. Of course, I don't remember that. Mom, my grandmother, told me.

I knew Gatha was different because she wore store-bought clothes like the city women wore in pictures in the magazines I saw. Sometimes she wore pants. Mom and Sybil made their own dresses from chicken-feed sacks with flowers printed on them and never wore pants. They didn't wear lipstick and smell fancy, nor did they drive a car. Only men drove cars, but Gatha drove like a man, as if she was born to do it, even if she did scrape a gear at times. She scared me and I didn't like her. It took me years to adjust to her. Maybe I never did. Taylor Swift says there is an ***"Invisible String"*** that binds us to others we love. I think she's right.

During World War Two my parents lived in a basement apartment in Washington, DC, and came every year to Leander for a long weekend to visit. Gatha would come on the train another time every year without Jennings, and stay for a week. In my mind, she was beautiful, like the women in the magazines. I could look, but I didn't want to touch. Mother wore lipstick and smelled like flowers. I was afraid of her, so I was cautious about her hugging me. Jennings wore fancy shoes and pants, different from the shoes and pants that Grandad ordered in the catalogue from Sears. Jennings talked differently, and didn't bother with me. I didn't speak to him, unless he asked me a question.

I was five or six years old before I really understood that these beautiful people were my parents, and even then, I wasn't sure about Dad. I had seen the card in Mom's Bible apparently announcing my birth, with a name that said Richard Allen Black. Who was that? Was that really me? Mom told me my last name was Roberts. But then, who was Richard Allen Black?

When she visited us, Gatha told me to call her "Mother," not Gatha. When I slipped a couple of times, she pinched my cheeks, and yelled at me, so I learned to call her "Mother," like she wanted. Mother tried to get me to eat tuna fish, spaghetti, and store-bought white bread, and other things Mom didn't grow or have. I rebelled. I was having none of that. She sat at the dining room table with me and tried to get me to switch from using my left hand to using my right hand. I wouldn't do that either. She tried to correct my pronunciation. I didn't change it. Was I spoiled? Of course I was.

Now, I realize this young mother was disappointed about having a child who wouldn't listen to her and was being raised by her mother in a remote mountain home that she had left even before high school. Her little boy was not yet three, walking around the farm by himself, barefooted, stepping in chicken manure. I think my mother and grandmother, Mom, were both flummoxed by the situation.

I believe Mom loved Gatha, but she couldn't deal with her. When Mom spoke to me about my mother, Mom's voice had a hint of sadness, mixed with a little anger, but laced in pretty language that I didn't notice her mood then. Mom's thoughts must have been something like this:

"***Gatha is my worst child. She's headstrong. She is nothing but an obstinate and rebellious child running wild. She's been wild all her life, even a lot worse than Sybil or Buddy. Sybil is sensible, and a good mother. Sybil married a coal miner who always has a good job. They bought a house close to us, and are doing a good job raising their three children.***

Gatha is always dressed up, and acts like she is some society woman. She's gone way above her raisings, AND she left her baby for me to raise. I do love him. Now he walks, and is always playing in the creek or running to the barn, and I'm too old to keep up with him. But now that he's getting older, I want to keep him. He can help

Melvin farm."

I never heard Mom complain, but I know that she felt that Gatha wasn't acting like an adult. Whenever one of Mom's neighbors walked up the road to visit her, she would send me outside or into my bedroom with a book, while they sat in the kitchen and talked, but seldom laughed.

Life As I Knew it

We lived just off of the Saturday road, on the Sunday Road in Leander, seven miles, as the crow flies, from the New River Gorge where the huge single-span arch bridge was built that is now a destination for tourists. It would be 15 or 20 miles if the crow had to walk. It was a remote and isolated part of West Virginia.

The house we lived in was one of the nicest in the area, but the standards in the area were ultra low. It was an unpainted, board-and-batten, one-story building built around 1900, that sat over a crawl space, with steps three feet up to a large front porch. The nearest electricity was three miles away in Ramsey. With no electricity, there was no plumbing, so we used an outhouse that was several yards from the house, but I peed in the front yard. In the winter, we used chamber pots, gallon-sized ceramic pots with lids, that were stored under the beds.

The bedrooms were always cold. In the fall, when it started getting cold, my grandparents moved their bed into the living room. I stayed in my bedroom sleeping under two or three handmade quilts. My bedroom window had a little piece of glass broken out, so every winter, if the wind blew when it snowed, I would wake up with snow on the foot of my bed. For cooling in the summer we opened the front and rear doors which had wooden screen doors. None of the windows ever opened.

All the inside light we had came through the windows during the day, and at night we burned two kerosene lamps for an hour or so, plus we had light from the fireplace when we had a fire in it. Yes, I read by the light from the fireplace like the historians say Lincoln did. So did every kid that read in the days before electricity.

I learned to read at an early age, because of the energy and time Grandad and Mom spent with me, holding me, and reading out loud from books, newspapers, and magazines even before I could follow along with the words. With Grandad reading Drew Pierson's newspaper column, ***The Washington Merry-Go-Round***. out loud, and me listening to Pierson on the radio, I learned about national affairs almost as soon as I could speak. I'll talk more about Drew Pierson a little later but I grew up thinking everyone followed national politics, as did Grandad's three children.

We weren't the poorest in the area, but we were poor. Of course, I didn't know that growing up there. We plowed and farmed with a horse. Life was just like it was in the 1740's, except Grandad had a pickup truck.

Our farmhouse sat back about 100 yards from the Sunday Road, a narrow dirt road that ran along the side of the hill across the creek. The creek ran through the flat land that held the barn at one end, a hundred yards from a big, old, white, two-story store building at the other end. The buildings are gone now, and trees have grown up, but the memories remain.

There was a board fence around the barnyard, with a gate that allowed trucks and equipment in and out of the barnyard. Grandad would take the chain off of a nail on the gatepost and open the gate to walk through. I was a climber, and explorer, so I climbed the four boards instead of opening the gate. I felt that was quicker, and more exciting.

Across the creek at the barnyard was a water gate. No, no, not a Watergate.That's what Nixon had. Ours was a water gate. Ours completed the fencing-in of the barnyard. This would allow the cattle to come into the creek to drink or stand in the water when it was hot.The gate was made with wooden pickets hanging down into the water across the creek, held in place about six feet above the water by a timber that was fastened to a post on either side of the creek in a way that would allow the timber to turn and allow some debris to pass through. There was a shorter log about six inches above the bottom of the pickets to provide stability. In a heavy rain the gate would swing enough to allow the water and smaller debris to pass through, but hold the large debris. Occasionally Grandad had to clear out the accumulation of larger pieces.

I was two or three when Grandad and a neighbor rebuilt the old foot bridge that spanned the creek where it ran across the yard in front of the house. He built an inclined ramp with rocks on one end and put a concrete surface on it. My head was lying on a pillow on the ramp shortly after dawn one morning, when the two Brackett boys who lived down the road came by, and saw me sucking on my heavy glass baby bottle while Mom was doing her laundry by the creek. I remember I had bitten the end of the nipple off, and was really just drinking it, not sucking, when one of the boys who was six or seven years old, saw me and came over and tickled me.

"Aah, the littl' baby's suckin' his bottle. You're too old to be doin' 'at," he said, teasing me.

I took his teasing to heart. I knew at that moment that I was ready to quit the bottle. It was my first time being shamed into changing my behavior, but not the last time. Since the Brackett boys moved away shortly after that, I never played with them. Sybil and her husband, Wink, and two children came on Sunday after church once a month, and I played with my cousins, Keith and Shirley who were both older than me,

Other than that, there were no children near, so I was a loner. I spent a lot of time playing on the footbridge and in the water in warm weather, since the water wasn't more than six inches deep where I played in the creek, unless there had been heavy rains. I rolled up my overalls and stood barefooted in the shallow water, picking up the rocks along the side of the creek to find crawdads that lived under the edges of the rocks. I would pick them up and talk to them, being careful that their pincers didn;t grab me. Under the bridge the creek was deeper, and full of minnows, so I stood on the bridge and spit in the water to watch the minnows come up and fight each other for position to see what had hit the water. When I threw my apple cores in the water it always started a major minnow madness.

At a low spot in the ground near the creek, an area would fill with water when it rained heavly, and leave fresh sand when the water went down. This was my sand box when it dried. I built miniature roads in the sand imagining myself running the roadbuilding equipment, and driving over the mountains with my toy cars, talking to myself about what new things I was doing. Perhaps I would play in the yard, lying in the grass, checking out the bugs and ants, or if they weren't around, looking at the grass and small weeds, as I dug in the dirt. Did I get dirty? You had better believe it. That's why Mom scrubbed my overalls.

During the day in the cold or rainy days, I would lie on the linoleum-covered floor in the living room, and play or look at pictures in Life Magazine before I could read. When the weather was warmer, I would lie on the floor of the front porch, or sit in the porch swing and read.

I liked exploring the inside of the old store building. An old side saddle was hanging on the wall that Mom had used when she rode horses years before. It was the only one I ever saw in my life. I stored rocks and things I had collected in an old cabinet that said "Clark" on the front in gold lettering. One day I opened the drawer and found a momma mouse giving birth to a family of babies. I quickly closed the drawer and came back a couple of days later. She had taken her family and left, probably to find a home with more privacy.

After I learned to read I spent a lot of time in the store building reading the stacks of old issues of Life Magazine, Redbook, Ladies Home Journal, Woman's Home Companion, and Reader's Digest magazines for hours. Before I could read I studied the pictures that were in Life Magazine, a weekly news magazine full of photographs that is still published but is now much different from those days. As I said, I saw the new issues in the house when they came in the mail. Life Magazine had pictures of beautiful women who wore lipstick and looked like my mother. I remember seeing one that was an advertisement of something, but the realistic-looking drawing was an overhead picture looking down on a man driving a convertible, with a woman who looked like Mother, standing in the car beside him, with both her and the man holding the steering wheel as she looked and smiled at the man. At age four or five, I knew that was fake. A woman standing on the floor of the car? Holding the steering wheel? Not looking where they were going? I knew I stood on the floor in the truck all the time, but I didn't hold the steering wheel. I held onto the dashboard, and I wasn't very tall. The woman in the picture would get bugs in her hair if that were real.

In the stacks of Life Magazine in the store building, there were hundreds of photographs of World War Two. The battle pictures were often grizzly and showed dead people. I learned what war was like from the pictures of the bombed buildings, the sad and worried expressions of the survivors, and the depressing pictures of the bombed cities in Europe. I don't remember hearing about the atomic bombs being dropped on Japan, but Life magazine had pictures that I saw. For a long time they would have pictures of the Japanese people who suffered skin burns, loss of limbs, and terrible radiation scars. Nagasaki was a town of 195,000, about the size of Birmingham, Alabama.They lost 40,000 people instantly, (about the size of Huntington, WV) but within four months they had lost another 30,000 people, (about the population of Morgantown, WV,) who had been injured. In Hiroshima, a city about the size of Winston Salem, NC, 25,000 men, women, and children died instantly. They had lost 75,000 people by Christmas. Imagine the grief in those cities. A couple of years later there were pictures of Japanese citizens.who were deformed from the burns, limbs distorted or missing. In America, during the war, we lost about 420,000 men and women (think Minneapolis). In almost any town in America, it was a common sight to see men missing an arm, or a leg walking with crutches. They wore shirts or pants with one sleeve or leg pinned up, or if no legs, he might be sitting on a quilt, on the sidewalk begging, or playing a harmonica or guitar for tips. If you don't believe me, ask someone over 80 about it.

The memories of those things stay with me today. May the world, and especially the USA, always be forever free from tyrants and people who disregard the moral and ethical principles of life. Keep us free from leaders who insult our citizens,and our global friends and foes, and who look to take other nations' territories. That's all I'm going to say about that.

We also felt the effects of WWII in our house. If we wanted to buy a pound of ground coffee, sugar, a tire, ten gallons of gasoline, canned foods, and lots of other things, we had to have a government-issued ration coupon for each unit we wanted to buy. They were as important in our lives as money. Every week before Grandad went to sell our surplus crops, Mom took the ration books out of the high dresser drawer where she kept them so I couldn't reach them. They discussed what they wanted to buy, and did we have the coupons to buy them, and did any store have sugar, or coffee. Maybe it would take two or three stores to find what they needed.

Right after the war had ended, one night Grandad stopped to get gasoline. Mom and I stayed in the truck. Grandad got back in the truck after he had gone in to pay.

"Here, I brought you two something," as he handed Mom a very small package.

"What is it?" I asked. She opened it, saying as she smiled,

"Lord, it's bubble gum. I haven't had any bubble gum since the war started five years ago." I had never heard of bubble gum..

"What's that?"

You chew it and you can blow bubbles. Here, take this and chew it."

I did, as she chewed and blew a big bubble.

"Stick your tongue in it and blow," she said.

"The war must be over if they're making bubble gum." Grandad said as I tried to make a bubble.

They were happy to find bubble gum. Lots of products had been unavailable for five or six years. As the war ended and factories could find supplies, and hire workers, the companies started making consumer items again. Before, if your car broke down, chances were high that you couldn't find parts, so you parked it. People born later than me don't understand the terrible consequences of a big war. Those my age do but younger people consider it just about old people getting older. If you were around during WWII, you remember it. The Korean and Vietnam wars weren't world wars. They were civil wars that America got involved in. They were terrible, but there was no shortage of bubble gum.

We saved scrap metal of any kind, even empty tin cans. Once a month a junk man would come by, take the scrap, and pay for anything he thought he could make a dollar on. The schools collected pods from the milkweed plant that grew around the area. They were bagged in a burlap bag and sent somewhere to be used to make life-preservers for the sailors. Now I realize my grandparents worried about my Uncle Buddy. Two months after the bombing of Pearl Harbor in Hawaii, The Japanese captured the Philippines and MacArthur was forced to leave. He went to Australia, where he famously said, "I shall return."

Uncle Buddy (Claude Ramsey) graduated from the University of Missouri with a degree in journalism, and became one of the PR people on MacArthur's staff, so he went with MacArthur to Australia. Buddy later wrote a book, ***From Generals to Gorillas***, a biography, written by him and his friend, the actor Betty White. In the book, he talks about his life with MacArthur, and him and Betty working together helping Dian Fossey, who was studying gorillas in Africa, when Buddy was Director of the Morris Animal Foundation, and Betty was a major donor.

My Early Education

Grandad was the teacher at Koontz, a one-room school two miles over the ridge, on the Sunday Road. After I turned four, he enrolled me as a student in the first grade at Koontz to learn, and I suspect, to get me out of Mom's hair. He read to all of us in the school from books like ***Gone With The Wind,*** and ***Grapes of Wrath,*** which are often banned now. The school did not have electricity. There was no well, so no plumbing. No one washed their hands at school. The boy's and girl's toilets were two square buildings painted green, about five feet square, with single seats over a deep hole in the ground. that sat on the hillside behind the school. Every Halloween one or both were turned over by someone. Every morning an eighth grade boy carried two regular galvanized buckets of drinking water from a neighbor's well, a tenth of a mile away, and poured it into a five-gallon ceramic urn.

The only heat came from a coal-burning stove in the center of the room.The potbellied stove was shielded behind a round, painted partition cover that stood about a foot away from the stove to keep the children from burning themselves. The protective hood would still burn anyone who touched it when the stove was very hot.

To get to Koontz School from the farm, Grandad and I, and the neighbor kids, walked the two miles in a group on the Sunday Road, up and down the steep ridge, and up and down smaller hills, lending credence to your grandparents telling you they "walked uphill to school both ways." Of course we walked downhill both ways too. In the warmer weather, most of us walked to school barefooted, as my mother had done when she was young. When it rained Grandad would drive the pickup truck, but many times we got wet. When he drove, he would fill the cab with four or five of us, usually the small ones got priority, and the rest would get in the back. Yes, they got wet, but they weren't in the rain as long as they would have been if they had walked. I don't think anyone had raincoats. No one I knew had an umbrella. There was no bus, other than the one that creeped the ten miles out the Saturday Road to Ansted, gathering high school students along the way. In a few years, I would come back and ride that bus to go to Ansted, but I'll tell you about that later.

One of our closest neighbors (a good half mile away) had four children, Gene, the oldest, Jack, the second, A.J., the third boy, and lastly, Sara Belle. Gene and Jack rode the bus into high school in Ansted. A.J. and I were friends. Sara Belle was a redheaded girl that I found fascinating, but we never bonded. I suppose Sara Belle was the reason that

I eventually married a redhead. I really liked her, but she didn't seem to be enamored with me, probably because she had three older brothers, who I'm sure tormented her. A.J. and I went to Koontz, but I don't remember Sara Belle being in school.

One cold frosty morning, when I was five or six, on the way to school, we stopped in the road at a little shanty to get Clyde, a schoolmate, who wasn't ready to join us. His mother stuck her head out of the door and called,

"Good morning, Mr. Ramsey. Clyde's not ready yet. Have Richard come in and get warm."

I ran in. The small house was heated with a small, hot, tin, wood stove in the center of the main room. As I stood by the stove next to Clyde's little sister, warming my hands I looked around. I could see there were only two rooms,one bedroom, and the living room with a cookstove and a table with chairs at one end. Since there were three children, I wondered where everyone slept. There was a bed in the crowded living room, so I deduced three children slept there, but maybe only two slept in the bed in the living room if one slept with their parents. The heat from the little stove was stifling, and the odor of urine coming from a vegetable can sitting on the floor by the hot stove was strong in the enclosed house. I never went back to his home, but I became aware that not everyone lived as fine a life as I did.

It was nice to have Grandad teach me for four years, (but through the fifth grade), even if he did spank me and another boy once for disturbing the class. Charlie (Fake name, because I don't remember it.) and I were standing in the back of the room by the water cooler having a drink of water from our notebook paper cups we had just made, while Grandad was teaching some eighth graders. Charlie and I were talking, giggling, and making noises by humming and blowing into the water with sounds coming out of our throats. We were obviously too loud, since Grandad stopped his lesson and called us to the front. As I stood there, he took his paddle and had Charlie bend over, as he spanked him hard three or four times. Then he had me bend over, and I got the same thing. I think it was the only time in life he ever spanked me. I was mortified. To add insult to injury, his paddle was part of one of my old toys where the paddle was attached to a ball by a rubber band. While we're discussing this, I'll tell you that Mom kept me in line by using a switch she would fashion from one of the bushes in the yard. I felt her wrath several times growing up.

My second year, since I was the only child in second grade, and there was only one boy in third grade, we two boys became the third grade class. With a birthday in October, I was five at the end of the third grade. I realize that now I was a pain in the posterior to the other kids. Walking to to school one morning, A.J., a couple of years older than me said to Grandad,

"Jim, him catched a rabbit last evenin." I immediately jumped in to correct him.

"No, don't say 'Jim him catched." He went quiet, but looked at me as if to say, "Shut up. I wasn't talking to you."

I said, "You're 'spossed to say, "Jim caught a rabbit. Don't say 'Jim, him,' neither."

I cringe today when I think of how bossy I was not, only

to my friends, but to everyone. To all of them, I apologize.

Not every lesson was learned inside of the one-roomed building. Judy Evans (Fake name) taught me some things outside of the building. Judy was an older woman who was practicing to be a caring mother, or a doctor. I don't know which. She was six years old, a year older than me, in the first grade. I was only five, in the third grade, but at my young age I fell prey to her older charms. One warm day at recess, she led me over to sit under a pine tree that had low hanging limbs and was located off the school property. When we sat down, we were hidden from everyone.

"Show me your 'thing,' and I'll show you mine." she said

I had to be certain about what she was looking for.

"What?"

She pointed downward.

"That!"

I complied, and she reciprocated. We checked each other out, until our curiosity was satisfied. In those few minutes we became better educated children. We kept our discoveries quiet, and we were never questioned or punished. We never repeated the incident, but I never forgot her name, or that moment.

That episode made me appreciate older women.

The women in the area made their dresses from cotton chicken feed bags that had small colored designs on them. The formless dresses were easy to make, and hid what they were supposed to hide, but were not very fashionable. These feed bags were a hold-over from the Depression days when most of the farm women in the country made clothes from them. Every girl I knew wore dresses made from the feed sacks with tiny flowers printed on them. Mom made her dresses and my shirts from them, operating her Singer sewing machine with her feet pumping the foot pedal. The bags had originally held one hundred pounds of chicken feed that Grandad bought, and that I would feed to the chickens, as soon as I was big enough..

The first time we wore a new item that our moms had made from the feed sacks the cloth was stiff and scratchy, and really felt uncomfortable, but we got used to it as the cloth softened some after it was washed a few times in the homemade lye soap that every family made,

Wash Day

Wash day was a hard day for Mom. Every week on wash day,at dawn, or before, Grandad went across the creek, built a fire, put the twenty-gallon bronze pot on a metal stand over the fire, and filled it with water from the creek. Then he went to the barn to feed the livestock and milk the cows. Mom put her apron on, started a fire in her stove, and fixed breakfast.

After breakfast, Mom washed the breakfast dishes in the sulphur-laden well water that we drank and only used in the house, since it stained everything it touched on a regular basis. (A new galvanized bucket and white dipper that we all drank from was a dull orange in a week or two), so she bundled the dirty laundry in a sheet, carried it across the creek, and dumped the clothes in the hot water with her homemade lye soap. She put a washtub on an old table, filled it with some hot water from the pot, and some cold water from the creek to lower the temperature. She stirred the laundry with an old, sawed-off broom handle, and in a couple of minutes took the clothes out of the hot kettle with the broom handle, and put them in the other tub where she checked to see if they needed scrubbing. If they did, she scrubbed them on a washboard in the tub she had filled. The washboard is a wooden-framed piece of corrugated, galvanized metal with irregular surfaces on it that will clean away dirt when you rub clothes over it. It also cleans away a lot of cloth, so it is not a perfect match. for the job. The work clothes, and my overalls usually needed scrubbing. Now, with computerized washing machines washboards are only used in New Orleans Jazz Bands. Seriously.

If the clothes did not need scrubbing, they went straight into a rinsing tub filled with creek water to get rid of the lye soap. My overalls would wear out in the knees from where they were scrubbed on a washboard. If they were torn, or there was a hole in the knee, they were not worn where someone might see them. Mom would cover the hole with a patch, and those could be worn on the farm, but not worn to school, even though other kids wore patches to school. Imagine the reaction older generation people and I had when the stores began selling new denim pants with holes and ripped places in them.

When all that was finished, Mom carried the clean laundry back over the bridge,and put the tub on a table on the side porch. Then she would run the clothes through the hand-operated wringer, a stand-alone piece of wooden equipment with two rubber rollers in the center that squeezed the water out of the clothes when the handle was turned. After running them through the wringer, she hung the clothes on the clothesline, a wire attached to a tree at one end and a clothesline pole at the other. After fastening the clothes on the line using wooden clothes pins, she took a pole about eight feet long with a notch in one end to hold the wire, and raised the line in the air so the dogs and I wouldn't get the clothes dirty while they dried. Hopefully, it wouldn't rain until after they had dried.

Mom ironed the clothes that needed to be ironed with an iron that had a wooden handle and two heavy, removable iron inserts. She ironed with one insert while the other heated on the stove and exchanged the two when the iron she was using cooled.

Even ice cream was hard work. When strawberries, peaches, raspberries or wild blackberries were ripe, Grandad would bring a block of ice home from a visit to Ansted, break it up in chunks and put it in the wooden ice cream maker, around a heavy metal container that had paddles inside. Mom made a mixture of milk, sugar, vanilla flavoring, and the fruit that was available. Grandad put the mixture into the inner steel container, and turned the paddles as he cranked the handle on top. It was too hard for me or Mom to turn, so Grandad turned it for ten or fifteen minutes and then checked to see that the ingredients had frozen. When he thought it was ready, the bowls and spoons came out. After he emptied the container, I was allowed to take my spoon to scoop out what he had left in. It seemed he could never get all of the ice cream out, so I always looked forward to scraping the container.

Grandad raised corn, potatoes, soybeans and sometimes buckwheat on twenty or thirty acres around the homestead. Five or six acres was an orchard that grew peaches and apples. One big black cherry tree stood at the end of one of the fields. Mom and Grandad planned and tended a large garden in the flat area just below the storebuilding for our use and for peddling, a term given to selling farm products off the back of the pickup to homeowners.

He owned another somewhat larger farm two miles down Richmond Chapel Road used for hay and summer pasture, that he called the "Other Place." Every spring we drove the cattle down the Sunday road to the intersection with the Richmond Chapel Road, where the "Boss Cow" turned right and led them past Richmond Chapel, and the cemetery, where my ancestors were buried. Every fall, we drove them back home. (They walked, as we "drove" them. Remember the westerns, where the cowboys went on "cattle drives"?) Almost every cow and calf followed the Boss Cow. If the Boss Cow wasn't in the herd another cow who had made the trip took over. I was severely reprimanded by my employer years later when I referred to the supervisor of our all-women accounting department, as "The Boss Cow." Don't ever do that.

Surveying and Writing Deeds

Since Granddad was the most educated person around the area, people would have him survey, mark the tract of land, and write the deed for the land they were selling. The nearest surveyor was thirty miles away in Fayetteville, and there was only one lawyer closer.

I went with him into the woods of someone's property and watched him pace off the number of yards to a corner and find a tree to put notches in with his hatchet, or place a big rock to mark the corner. Often there was a tree nearby, and he would put chop marks unless it had been marked--and usually it had not. A different number of notches meant something different. (Today, especially in the South, there still are streets named “Two-Notch Road,” or “Three-Chop Road,” signifying old property markings for ownership of land.) Then, turning in whatever next distance was needed, using the surveyor’s tool in his mind, paced off the angle and distance to the next corner, where the procedure would repeat itself. If he was off 20 or 30 feet, it really didn’t matter. The buyer bought what Granddad said he bought.

At home, I watched him write out the description of the tract of land by hand from his notes using strange (to me) legal words like “thence.” Then he would pull a pack of papers with a heavier blue paper on the outside from his drawer, open it up and handwrite the deed in ink, using strange words again, like, “whereas,” “warrant,” and “henceforth,” to signify selling the land to whomever the owner wanted to sell the property to. It occurred to me later in life that my mother must have watched the same thing. Maybe that’s why she fell in love with a boy who wanted to be an attorney. How much did this cost the seller? Maybe five dollars. If they were “on the dole,” (collecting welfare, and a lot were), perhaps a couple of chickens, or two bushels of sweet potatoes that he could sell on Saturday on his peddling route.

If I was at home after the mailman went by in his shiny green truck, Mom would say,
“Buddy, run across the creek and get the mail.” She often called me “Buddy.”
I would run (I ran everywhere) across the creek, and up the hill to the big red mailbox and bring back the “goodies,”

(magazines, or a package from Sears). If I brought back a package, my question was, "Is there something in here for me?" If it was a magazine like Life, Ladies Home Companion, or Ladies Home Journal, she would sit in her painted rocking chair and read. (She and Grandad each had matching wooden rockers with woven bottoms.). If she was up to date on reading her magazines, she would put her head back, close her eyes, and softly sing to herself songs like ***"The Old Rugged Cross."***

The Tractor and Truck

Around the time I was eight, Grandad took me thirty miles across the mountains to Rainelle to visit the International Harvester Dealer that served our area. While in Rainelle he showed me the high school that Mother and Sybil had attended and where they had rented a room. Why did they go to school in Rainelle, and not closer to home? I don't know. Perhaps that was the closest High School a hundred years ago. Mother told me she spent a summer making beds and cleaning rooms at the Greenbrier Hotel. Maybe it was when she was in high school.

Grandad ordered a Farmall Super "A" tractor with a six-foot-sickle-blade mower, plow, cultivator, and disc harrow, from Gilkerson, the dealer who delivered the bright red tractor one evening. I thought it was beautiful. He and his son stayed into the late night, using lights on the tractor and trucks to assemble and teach Grandad and me the proper installation and assembly of the various implements.

I quickly learned how to drive the tractor, and I was

allowed to cultivate the crops in the fields on top of the hills around the house, and mow at the "Other Place" by myself with no one around. I cultivated barefoot, but wore shoes when I was mowing because the cut stubs of the tall grass sticking out of the ground stabbed my feet when I got down from the tractor to clean the mower blades, or do any sort of adjustment. More than once, I mowed the eight acre field at the Other Place and never saw any one while I did it in a day.

I learned the basic elements of maintenance, and mechanics of the equipment and the truck. I learned to drive the truck by driving it in the fields to gain experience, and soon I was driving it on the roads, first from the house to the Other Place, or Ramsey, and soon after, to the Midland Trail, with Grandad beside me. Once when I was nine, I met a Deputy Sheriff where we both had to pull to the side of the Saturday Road to pass. I stopped to let him drive by. As he came past, we made eye contact but we both drove on. I was immensely relieved when he didn't stop me.

Peddling Produce

On Friday nights we loaded the truck with the farm products to sell to coal miners' wives in the mining communities near Montgomery. There might be ten or twelve gallon jugs of buttermilk, and five or six pounds of butter, ten to fifteen dozen eggs, some cabbage, tomatoes, green beans, cucumbers, ears of corn, and cantaloupes, strawberries, and occasionally rhubarb from a single plant on top of a hill. Later in the year we offered apples, sweet potatoes, Irish potatoes, turnips, parsnips, occasionally grapes, and horseradish that was grown under the grape arbor in the side yard. Every year, in the late fall after butchering, we always sold the head of the hog that we had butchered, all wrapped up in a sheet for cleanliness and sanitation. We brought the sheet home with us after it was sold.

With all these foods available, I learned to eat and enjoy them, even the horseradish. I learned to eat a very small amount each time mixed in something, instead of eating a big chunk of horseradish at once. I learned that lesson when I bit into a solid piece of horseradish, it burned my mouth like never before, or since. Being a smart child, I never did that again.

Saturday mornings we got "dressed up," which meant clean overalls, and shoes and socks for me. Grandad wore a suit if it wasn't too hot, but at least a dress shirt, tie, and pants with suspenders. If Mom went, she would wear one of the two dresses she had bought from Montgomery Ward. At dawn we left the house.

Grandad would stop and pick up whoever was walking along the road, usually, one or the other of the two different men who lived just off the Saturday road, and didn't have a car. These two men's cornbread wasn't completely baked. In West Virginia language, that means they lacked mental capacity. They lived with their elderly mothers, and in Grandad's eyes were believed to be honest, but he wasn't entirely sure. If Mom were with us, they had to sit in the bed of the truck. He took them out the Saturday Road and turned right on Rt 60, and dropped them off in Victor or Ansted and continued on the Midland Trail, and down the mountain to Gauley Bridge, often meeting the morning Greyhound with Richmond plastered across the top of the bus in the space for the destination, as it headed east. As he crossed the Gauley river, I always looked at the old stone piers that held the first Gauley Bridge where Bartholomew Ramsey, the first Ramsey to live in this area, worked as a stone mason in the 1820s, building the piers that supported the covered wooden bridge that first crossed the Gauley River. The bridge was captured three times, during the Civil War, and was burned, rebuilt, and burned, but my ancestor's stonework still stands, over 200 years later, guarding the river like a sentry.

We drove through Glen Ferris, and Alloy, both steel mill towns, but going past Glen Ferris we drove close to the mill, where I could see the steel workers working around the intense fire, and hear the machinery clanging and banging. That may have been one of the reasons I worked in the steel industry for forty years.

At Montgomery we crossed the bridge and turned left to follow the river back upstream on the south side along the railroad tracks. I always looked forward to crossing the river, since tugs would be pushing barges full of coal and steel down the river or bringing something up river to the steel mills in the towns we had passed through.

A couple of miles outside of Montgomery, he would start making stops around Kimberly, sometimes trying a house he had never sold before, but usually the customers were the same week after week. This is where I learned to count, multiply, and figure out the exact change in my head, while standing in the back of the pickup. I also learned to be a salesman, not necessarily a good one, but I was happy to just be a young salesman.

I carried the jugs of buttermilk, butter, eggs, or whatever, up the steps to the houses on the hills and collected the quarters, and maybe an empty glass milk jug (actually they originally had been one gallon Coca-Cola syrup bottles sold to drug stores for fountain drinks.) The miner's wives were always kind and nice to me, and I enjoyed seeing their clean kitchens with electrical and gas appliances that I marveled over. One woman's kitchen had an electric clock made like a black cat, hanging on the wall. As the seconds went by the cat's tail went back and forth. Another had a cuckoo clock hanging on the wall. Early on, Mom came with us, but later when I was big enough to help a little, and not be a problem, she stopped going.

Making Lumber

One of the things that brought me pleasure was going with Grandad and another man to find a tree to cut down, for whatever purpose. Maybe logs for cash, maybe logs to be cut for lumber in the kitchen remodeling. We would tromp through the woods , exciting in its own right, looking up at the trees, judging whether they were the right type of wood, were they straight enough, big enough, or straight enough. If the tree was "nigh on to perfect," then I could watch the cutting of the tree. There was nothing like being in the woods, smelling fresh sawdust, and watching the men saw through a hardwood tree. There were no power saws. To cut down a tree, the sawyers would notch the tree in the direction they wanted the tree to fall and with two men holding on each end of a six-foot-long saw, each man would pull the saw in a rhythm that was interesting to watch, but too hard for me to do for more than a couple of minutes. The sawyers would start sawing from the back side of the notch, until the tree was severed, and it would fall in the direction of the notch. Not always, but usually if the sawyers were experienced.

Often Grandad was on one end of the saw. As he was older, he would stop sawing quicker than most sawyers. to rest for a moment. The person on the other end of the saw would have to stop, since it was a two man saw. Grandad would tell a story or recite a limerick. After receiving a laugh from those around him and catching his breath he would continue sawing.

Grandad had a good sense of humor and loved to tell stories. My mother inherited this love, and I guess I have it too. I remember one of his limericks went like this:

"A boy stood on the burning deck,

" Eating peanuts by the peck.

"A little girl, who no one knew,

"Said, 'I wish I had a peck or two.'"

He never repeated this limerick in the house, or school. When the tree was on the ground, the men would either saw or chop the limbs off, using a saw or an axe. The tree would be cut in standard lengths, depending on what the order called for, and depending on the diameter of the log. The larger logs would be cut shorter to take the weight into account for the truck. When the tree was "dressed," or I suppose to be exact, "undressed," with the limbs removed, the men would hitch a horse to the logs, and drag them to a spot where they could get the logs rolled onto a truck.

When there was a truckload, the trucker brought his truck up the mountain trail (not good enough to be called a road), usually a two-ton truck with a sixteen-foot flat bed on the back. He parked in the right spot where the men used the slope of the hillside and manually rolled the logs on the truck using tools called Peaveys or Cant Hooks. (spelled correctly.)The trucker would chain the logs on and slowly drive down the logging road to the main road. He would haul the logs to the sawmill, sometimes close by, sometimes several miles away depending on the desires of the log's owner and the location of the desired sawmill.

For a couple of years there was a sawmill within a mile of where we lived. It was exciting for me to go with Grandad to visit the sawmill and watch the men cut flat boards out of round trees. There was a large four-foot circular saw mounted on an axle, with a pulley. Ten or fifteen feet away was a truck motor, complete with transmission and gear shift that drove a pulley turning the flapping belt that went to the saw. There was also the bed that carried the logs to the saw, and returned to have the new board unloaded, and to adjust the log for the next board. The boards were stacked on top of each other in piles with strips of wood between the layers to allow the boards to dry out or cure. All of this was before government regulations on workplace safety, think OSHA. There were no guards anywhere on the saw, the belts, or the traveling bed, so it was dangerous for me, just standing back and watching, as well as the workers.

Not all trees were cut for lumber. We also cut smaller trees, normally pine trees, typically in five-foot lengths as posts to be used inside the coal mines, to keep the roofs of the mine from collapsing on the workers. The posts varied in diameter depending on the tree, from four to six inches. The coal mine companies were continually buying mine timbers, to hold the mine open. and they fed many West Virginia families with their mining post purchases.

When Grandad had the kitchen and dining room remodeled after the advent of electricity, he cut specific types of trees for specific purposes, and had the boards cut in a couple of sawmills.

He stored cherry, hickory, maple, and oak lumber in the store building to dry out. After it dried, he loaded some of it in the '38 Chevy, and I went with him to a planing mill near Beckley to get the boards smoothed. It was a long trip, down the mountain, to Chimney Corner, across the New River on Rt. 19 before the new bridge was built, and up the other side, through Fayetteville and Oak Hill, to a town called Beaver. Beaver is now on the edge of Beckley, but then it was a very small town outside of the city, on its own.

At the planing mill, the air was filled with the scent of fresh wood, and I enjoyed standing near the equipment watching the planing mill throw off the shavings and smelling the cherry boards they were planing. They unloaded our boards and during the next week they would put the boards through the planing mill that planed off the saw marks and made them into finished wood that could be used to make furniture. The next week after they unloaded our rough boards they would reload the work they had done the week before. We would come back in a week with a new load and pick up the last week's load that had been finished.

We did this a few times, but then with a louder and

louder voice, the pickup started complaining by growling and fussing about the trip and the weight. On a return trip with a full load on the truck Granddad pulled into the Chevrolet garage in Oak Hill, and the mechanic said that the rear gear had worn out and a total failure was imminent.

It was late in the day, and nothing could be done until the next day, so the mechanic, who lived in Fayetteville, offered to drive us to Aunt Sybil's house in Lansing, across the New River at Fayette Station, three miles past his home, as the crow flies, but well over an hour to drive, since he had to drive sixteen long miles to Lansing, and sixteen miles back to Fayetteville.

Grandad accepted his kind offer, and we got in the mechanic's new '48 Chevy sedan. I sat in the back with my eyes focused on the front, watching the mechanic drive this fancy car. Going down the narrow mountain road (with no guard rails!) to Fayette Station, he held the steering wheel with his knee while he took a cigarette out of the pack and lit it with his Zippo cigarette lighter. I was mesmerized. This man was driving down the mountain holding the steering wheel with his knees. He was not in any tight turns, but I had never seen this before. It was a procedure I never forgot, but often used.

A Look At My Future

The summer I was eight, Mother came and took me on the train to visit Washington, DC, for three or four days. I was excited to go on the trip, because it was my first train ride, and I knew from the magazines I had read that there was a world out there that I had never seen. When

I got there I didn't like DC. The big city overwhelmed me. There was a lot of traffic, lots of noise, people and buildings everywhere. The sirens blared all night. The gas stove in the kitchen smelled bad, and the water tasted horrible. The apartment was small. There was a tiny front yard that had other children playing in it. I hardly knew my mother, and I knew Dad even less, but I knew I didn't like them. They were strict, and kept telling me what to do, or what not to do.

Until that trip I never knew I had an older half-brother, Jerry, who was six years older than me. Jerry had type 1 diabetes. He weighed his food before he ate it, and once a day, gave himself a shot of insulin in his hip. I had never spent any time with two-year-old Jim, my younger brother. Dad put all of us in his '47 Oldsmobile and showed us the beauty of the city. Unfortunately, I couldn't appreciate the idea of a beautiful city. I knew I could never live in DC. Mark Twain once said, **"It ain't what you don't know that gets you into trouble. It's what you know for sure that just ain't so,"** but I didn't know that then.

After my fourth grade at Koontz, Grandad was assigned to teach at Minter, a one-room school beyond Ramsey, off of the Saturday Road. Since it was more than three miles away that meant he drove every day. Of course I went with him. I didn't like going to Minter. Grandad apparently didn't either because he retired from teaching after teaching that one year in Minter. Grandad's brother, Anson, was teaching at Cavendish, a one room school near our house, so, that fall, when I was eight, I started sixth grade in Great Uncle Anson's, one-room school, Cavendish. I turned nine that October. I was happy. But stay tuned. Taylor Swift said it best:***"Time, mystical time. Cutting me open, then healing me fine."***

My father had become an attorney for the CAA, (now the FAA) dealing with regulations for airplanes and airports, so Mother and Dad bought a tall row house in the 400 block of 10th Street, NE, only ten blocks from the .Nation's Capitol, Mother wanted me to come live with them, because they had room for me, and I would lose the ways of a backwoods person, and learn to live a normal life. Also, I could help around the house when Mother had her new baby. My grandparents resisted. Grandad took me with him to visit Gatha's first husband, Mr. Black, who was, I discovered, manager of a woman's clothing store in Charleston. Mr Black took Grandad into his office and closed the door, while I waited outside his office by putting my feet into a fluoroscope x-ray machine in the shoe department and checking my toes. Shortly, the man and Grandad came out of the office. He and I looked at each other for a long moment. He turned away, and as he left, he said with disgust,

"I don't want anything to do with him. He's not my boy."

I didn't want anything to do with him either. He didn't look friendly to me, and he growled, so I was happy with the outcome. The next day, Grandad went by himself to see an attorney about getting custody of me. He was told he wouldn't win. Mother would prevail. My life was about to get screwed up in a major fashion, but maybe, **"What doesn't kill us makes us stronger."**

Part Two

WASHINGTON, DC

I was nine that spring in 1949 when I finished sixth grade at Cavendish. When school was over, Dad drove in and picked me up. I had my clothes in a cardboard box, but I did not take any pictures, toys, balls, or my bicycle. I just had a box of clothes and a churning stomach. I sat and cried silently, as this man I hardly knew tried to talk to me. I was upset, mad, and scared, so he gave up and quit trying. He drove to Ohio, where I met relatives that I had no idea I had, including my other grandmother, Dad's mother. Dad was taking her to DC to help Mother through the birth of her third baby.

We spent the night at Dad's sister's, my new (to me) aunt's, farmhouse, near Hillsboro, east of Cincinnati. Dad gave me a new raincoat he had brought. I was wearing it in the rain when I went into the barn with my new cousin, Joe. I brushed against an old piece of farm equipment and got a grease stain on the raincoat. When I came back into the house, Dad saw it. He raised his voice,

"Look at you! You've got grease all over that brand new raincoat! How the hell did you do that?!"

I was on the verge of crying in front of these new people, but the tears stayed in. So did the terrible memory.

The next day we picked up my "new" grandmother and returned to DC. A pickup truck sideswiped us on a two-lane highway, in West Virginia, and badly scraped up the left side of Dad's '48 Nash. I somehow felt that the car crash represented the crash in my personal life.

All of the impressions of my first trip to Washington revisited me at the new house. But this time, there was no going back home. There was still a tiny front yard, but no one played in it. On this street, the traffic wasn't so bad. The sirens still screamed all night. My half-brother, Jerry, didn't live there. The water was still terrible. The odor from the stove wasn't so bad. Here, the streetcar came from downtown less than a block from the house on "D" street and went downtown a block away on "C" Street. The house was a lot bigger than the apartment they had lived in before. This time there was a backyard with fences between us and our two neighbors. But my heart ached for my old home and grandparents. I was scared and lonely, so that night I cried.

Black and white TV was a wonderful distraction from my screwed-up life. I had never seen a television set before. Color TV hadn't been invented then, but any TV was a wonderful new thing for me. Here were shows just for kids, like Howdy Doody, and The Lone Ranger. The Kukla, Fran and Ollie Show was on every weeknight. There were movies where you could see complete old westerns. I had never seen a western movie before. Men rode horses in the movies like they did in West Virginia. Dad liked to watch those with us. One time after the movie that the family was watching was over, Dad asked me,

"Did I ever show you where the horse kicked me?"

"No," I said.

He held the palm of his hand toward me, pointed to the bottom of it with a finger from his other hand, and hit me with the lower part of his palm on my forehead, hard, but not terribly hard. Child abuse? I guess people would call it that today, but it was funny to everyone including me, even though it hurt for a few minutes. All of us laughed, but after that, Jim and I always said “yes!” when he asked again and again..

On TV there were comedians, like Milton Berle, and even old friends like Jack Benny, and Bing Crosby, who I had heard on the radio. There were four TV stations broadcasting from DC in 1949: NBC on channel 4, WTTG, the Dumont Channel, on channel 5, ABC on channel 7, and CBS on channel 9. Channel numbers 1-12 were printed on all TV cabinets. No channels were higher than 12.

Of course there were no remote controls to change channels. Dad would have me get up and change the channels, unless the picture quality needed to be adjusted. I didn’t know how to adjust for the best picture, because there were three or four controls on the front of the TV for adjusting it since the picture quality varied at times, I never saw it happen, but about midnight, the station would play the ***Star-Spangled Banner,*** go off the air, and put on a still picture called a test pattern that had each station’s ID with fine lines that could be used to fine-tune your picture. In 1949, the stations wouldn’t start broadcasting until four or five the next afternoon, so I heard the ***Star-spangled Banner***, and saw the test patterns then. I suppose the station’s engineers worked on the transmitters at that time to adjust the quality of the picture they were broadcasting.

One of the people we often saw on TV then was Dagmar. One headline called her “West Virginia’s Nearly Forgotten Glamour Girl.” Dagmar can best be described as Marilyn Monroe before her time. Dagmar usually played the “Dumb Blonde” role, but apparently, like Marilyn, she only acted that way because it paid well. Mom would always tease Dad about her when Dagmar appeared on a show, telling Dad,

"There's your girl. I'm going to have to leave, so you two can get together."

She never left his side, but she always said it before she snuggled into him on the couch. Dad would smile, but never said anything.

Dagmar was nine years younger than Mom, and dressed like a glamour girl, but I really think Mom would score higher than Dagmar if there ever was a direct competition with Dagmar. Oh, I didn't tell you all of it? Ok. Here it is.

Well, Dagmar lived in a tiny, wide-place-in-the-road called Yawkey,WV, less than ten miles from Hamlin where Dad and Mom both taught in the two room elementary school. In those small communities it wasn't unusual for a bus to be picking up kids who lived along the road, and hauling some of them as much as 20 miles. I'll tell you about Jim and I riding 15 miles to an elementary school later. It also was not unusual for a young person to be teaching school. They had a sixteen-year-old teaching at Koontz after Grandad left to teach at Minter. Check out **"Little House on the Prairie."** They had Mary teaching in a one-room school. Dad had not graduated from college then, because he couldn't afford it. He graduated years later. Dagmar would have gone to elementary school when Mom and Dad taught in Hamlin. Did those three people know each other?? Who knows.

The family who lived on one side of us had a giggly, bouncy, nine-year old daughter, named Karen. Karen and I became good friends through the months, as we stood on our sides of the four-foot high fence and talked and joked with each other. We questioned each other relentlessly, since our backgrounds were so totally different. I was white, and from raw wilderness-type country. She was black, and a city girl. She and I went to different schools because the court decision in ***Brown vs Board of Education*** to consolidate schools wouldn't happen until 1954, and segregation was a very real thing with arguments on either side by adults. As the weeks went by, we became close friends, and we would touch hands and let our fingers linger touching each other through the woven metal fence. I was pleasantly surprised when she kissed me on the cheek. Did I kiss her? I really don't remember, but I probably did. None of our parents seemed to worry about our talking and playing together. Neither of us ever went into the other's yard, since there was no common gate, and we would have to go through the locked garages, or through the houses. I don't know why we never went out front where there was no fence.

Even with all the new things, or because of some of them, that summer I cried in bed most nights. I didn't like the food. I felt Mother was cruel and too tough on me. Often, I had to clear the table and wash the dishes. I had to make my bed and change my and Jim's sheets using hospital corners every week.Does everyone know about hospital corners? No? Well.I didn't either, but I learned. Apparently Mother had to use them when she worked her way through college as a housekeeper in various places, including the Greenbrier Resort in White Sulphur Springs.. She would check to be sure I had made them properly. In West Virginia, my chores had been to gather the eggs, feed the chickens, get the mail from the mail box, bring coal ion to the house, feed the stove when it needed it, empty the ashes, but never to wash dishes, change bed sheets, or sweep the floor. To me, these chores weren't my job. It never occurred to me that we didn't have any of those chores now. Learning how to do these chores did teach me how to be self-sufficient, a trait that would prove to be very useful to me the rest of my life.

Remembering Sybil's big noisy Hoover, I hated my job of vacuuming with an old Electrolux vacuum cleaner with a big metal tank that slid on chrome runners as you used it. Every week on Saturday mornings, I vacuumed the entire second floor and the stairs with the Electrolux clunking down the stairs behind me, then I scrubbed the bathroom. Mother came behind me to inspect my work and fuss at me if I missed something. I missed the farm, my grandparents, all the animals, the dogs, the cats, the cows, the chickens, even the pigs. That's what I missed. I knew living here in the city wasn't for me. What did you say, Mark Twain, **"It's what you know for sure that just ain't so"?**

Mother's language bothered me. I thought she talked like some of the men in West Virginia. One of her favorite cuss words was s**t. If I said I wanted something that I wasn't going to get, she would say:

"Put your wants in one hand and s**t in the other and see which one fills up quicker." If she was being sarcastic, she might say "Hot Spit."

I made up stories in my mind. For example, stories about Mother making me a cake and smiling at me, but it never happened. I realize now that the last trimester of a pregnancy can be difficult, especially with an unhappy nine year old boy in the house.

Jim and I shared a room upstairs in the back of the house. My "new" grandmother had a room on the first floor, until she returned to Ohio, when Jan was a month or so old. Mother and Dad slept in the big bedroom upstairs overlooking Tenth Street.

Dad worked hard to bring me into his family. I'm fairly certain Mother made him do it, and now I feel that he probably resented having to bring me into his small family, but I don't really know. First, he took me alone to Glen Echo, the DC area's amusement park one evening, to enjoy some father-son time. Now, I see what he was doing, but I didn't see it then. My feelings for him were still hurting from his up-rooting me from my grandparents, and my awe of him because of his strict demeanor, and harsh voice. I rode the merry-go-around while he watched, then together, we went into the hall of mirrors, and a haunted house. I enjoyed it but the uneasy feelings were still there.

In a little while, (days? weeks? months? I don't know.) he took me to see the Washington Nationals baseball team. I generally knew how baseball was played from playing softball at recess in the one-room-school days, but this was different. We sat in the bleachers, a long way from home plate, but it was a new experience for me, and I was getting to know the city.

Mother took Jim and me downtown a couple of times to show us which stores to go in, and where to catch the 13th and "D" streetcar to come home on. Then she let Jim and me go downtown by ourselves. We would go down and maybe buy socks, or underwear, shopping at Hecht's, or Woodward & Lothrop, two of the major department stores. We thought we had grown-up when she let us do that.

After Mother took me shopping for groceries two or

three times, one of my jobs became buying groceries. I liked that. I enjoyed being away from her, on my own, learning new things, learning to think, making decisions, and dealing with adults around me. I didn't know then, but she was teaching me responsibility and how to shop so when the baby was born she wouldn't have to go to the stores.

She trained me in what brands to buy, and to keep the money in a safe place until I checked out. I pulled Jim in our red wagon, like the one every boy owned, down "E" St. to the Acme grocery store on 15th St. Outside the store four or five boys with wagons were lined up along in the front, waiting to haul groceries for women. Jim and I went in, and we selected the items on our list. I paid for them, we went out and put them in the wagon and went home. No problems. Until.... One day when I went to check out, I couldn't find the ten dollar bill Mother had given me. Since ten dollars was like a hundred dollars today, I was terrified. Jim and I went home and I told Mother. She looked at me with anger in her eyes, and let out cuss words. She searched me and finally found it in a sweater pocket under my coat that I had missed. We both smiled, me more than her, and I hurried back to the store to pay and collect my groceries. One of the things I always bought was her Herbert Tareyton cigarettes. Remember that brand? I didn't think so. I don't know if the laws have changed, or if they had the laws and no one enforced them, but I don't think stores will sell cigarettes to a nine-year old today. In those days, cigarettes were for sale everywhere in vending machines so anyone could buy them, but they were expensive in the vending machines. A pack of cigarettes from the machines cost a quarter.

Edmonds elementary school was around the corner at ninth and D, but Mother enrolled me in Maury Elementary, at Constitution Ave and 13th Street, NE, eight blocks away. Maury had a kindergarten for Jim. Mother and Dad correctly assumed that at my age of nine, going on ten, and my being raised in the backwoods of West Virginia, I was not mature enough to attend a middle school in DC. I was only a little unhappy about that, I thought it was unnecessary to have to repeat the sixth grade. I would find out shortly that I was wrong. This sixth grade was totally different. And, by not going to the closest elementary school, I could walk Jim to school, because the closest school did not have a kindergarten class.

I can't explain to anyone how everything affected me living in DC. It was so totally different from the way my life had been before I was uprooted. I missed playing with the cows and calves, the cats and dogs, even looking at the pigs, playing in the creek, the smell of Grandad when he wore his old jacket to the barn to milk. But, as school started, I adjusted to a totally new school. My life got better. I was away from the house and in charge of my life a lot more. The crying stopped. The water tasted better. I had a friend at home, Karen. I had friends at school, and a lot of people I could interact with, including the cashiers at the Acme store. I started calling my mother "Mom." Sometimes she showed that she loved me, and talked to me as an adult. School was interesting. My brother was a nice guy, but stubborn, so gleefully, I became the alpha dog, and so I picked on him as we walked the eight blocks to school every day, wearing raincoats with hoods, when it rained. No umbrellas for us. In the winter, Jim and I played in the dark basement lit with a couple of lightbulbs hanging from the ceiling close to the wire clothes lines for Mother. Jim had gotten a Lionel model train for Christmas so we set it up and played C&O Railroad. What are the rules for C&O Railroad? Who knows. Heck, you can make them up, but it does involve train wrecks.

I had a good friend in my class named Trenton, a red-headed boy, with a face full of freckles, who came home with me a few times, since he was a "latchkey kid" (meaning he went home to a locked, empty house while his mother worked). Mom fell in love with him. Trenton was so very polite, and used phrases like,

"Yes, Ma'am" and "Thank you, Ma'am."

After he left, Mom said,

"Why can't you be nice like Trenton?"

What she didn't know was that Trenton had a side job of stealing hubcaps and hood orniments from cars parked on quiet streets, and selling them to his fence. I knew that dog wouldn't hunt, so I just bit my tongue.

I only went into three people's homes while I lived in DC. Two of them were Mother's friends, the third one was Irving's. I don't remember why, but I went home with him one day, and I saw that his family lived just like we did; so I began to understand that the way we were living was the way other families with kids my age lived. I had a good friend named Clarence, but we never visited each other's homes. Other than Trenton, none of my friends ever came to my house. Remember, my school was outside our neighborhood, so none of my schoolmates lived near me.

I was sorry that Judy didn't live closer to me. Judy lived on the opposite side of the school from me, so I never saw her except in class or the school yard. Judy, and I had a somewhat secret mutual crush on each other. To be exact, the mutual crush was real. Our secret was "somewhat secret." In the school yard we stood close to each other and talked about things as I looked into her pretty eyes. No, I don't remember what color. Probably blue. Often, we touched hands. Sometimes she would run and I would have to run to catch her and hold her tight. She made my insides feel good with our touching, holding, and talking, and I'm certain she felt the same way, but we never talked about it. I got a heavy ration of trash talk from a couple of my classmates who watched us playing together every day, but we kept the relationship going as long as I went to Maury. (BTW, no one knew what "trash talk" was back then. Those words came from professional basketball when TV began carrying it. Still, we boys in the sixth grade all knew for a fact that girls had cooties. What did you say, Mark Twain? "**It's what you know for sure that just ain't so?"**

I liked the totally different curriculum in school here. There were no old Elson Readers, as there had been in West Virginia. The textbooks were current, and we had an art project, where each student in my room carved lines in an asbestos floor tile to make a pattern. (Asbestos was used in floor tiles until the mid seventies.) I carved a sailboat that was on a lake in Ecuador, a country we studied. Then we rolled ink on our patterns and printed them on cloth to make small tablecloths for our parents. I wrote essays about things like the brand-new United Nations, Ecuador, and Sonja Henia. None of these things were ever mentioned in Cavendish School.

Miss Williams assigned us a project to research and write a report in ink, about "someone famous," and for some unknown reason, Mom insisted it be about Sonja Henia, an Olympic skating star from the '30's who was now a movie star in America, making movies with her skating. She once said she "wanted to do on skates what Fred Astaire did dancing." Watch Sonja skate on YouTube. She was like Caitlin Clark, just a different kind of athlete.

It was my first time writing in ink, and I had a lot of trouble writing with a fountain pen. For one thing, if I pressed the pen down too hard, the ink would run all over the paper. Ball point pens were around, but were still very expensive, so only a few people used them. I "blotted" what I wrote by placing a special piece of absorbent paper called a blotter" on the wet ink. A blotter usually had printing on one side with advertising from an insurance or real estate company. The blotting kept it from running, but if the paper became smudged, or ink got where it wasn't supposed to be, Mother would make me copy the whole page over. It seemed the smudges always happened after I had written most of the page. The only way to remove ink from the paper was to dab it with a small amount of bleach on a cloth which stank, and anyone could tell that ink had been erased.

Ink was sold in small glass bottles. When I needed to put ink in my pen, I pulled up a tiny lever that was on the barrel of the ink pen, which depressed a rubber bladder inside the barrel of the pen. When I stuck the pen down into the bottle, covering the bottom of the pen in the ink, and released the lever, the pen sucked the ink into the bladder in the pen. It was a precarious task, and the whole process was one that I dreaded. The ink in the pen might last a full page. At some point that year, I turned a bottle of ink over and made a horrible mess. I don't remember if it was that report, or another, but I cried when I did that.

Sometimes on Saturdays after I vacuumed the upstairs, and Jim and I had lunch, we were allowed to walk down to 13th and "H" streets to the one-o'clock-Saturday-afternoon-movie matinee. We never saw anyone we knew there. Mom gave each of us a quarter to get in, and a dime to buy our snack, or drink. The movies started with a serial movie that was continued from week to week, always ending with the hero captured, tied up, or in great peril. The following week, he (or she) would find a way out or was saved from their troubles from last week, and continue on to fight for law and order. But in fifteen minutes, the hero was in another life-threatening situation, to be solved next week.

There usually would be a cartoon movie, perhaps where Wile E. Coyote would set a trap for the Roadrunner, a bird that lived on the ground in the Southwest, who would turn the tables and the box of dynamite would explode in Coyote's face, leaving it all dark with smoke or ashes, but Coyote would still be alive.

Then the movie started. It was often a western in black and white left over from the late thirties, or maybe a feature-length film with Dagwood Bumstead and Blondie, played by human actors. There were no color movies in the matinees. Color movies were saved for after 6:00 PM one-dollar admissions.

At Maury I became a safety patrol officer. I was given a white safety patrol belt that went over my shoulder and fastened around my waist. I pinned my patrol officer's metal badge on it. My first week I stood on the sidewalk at 12th place and Constitution and let the children cross. 12th place is a very quiet street, and the teacher could stand in our classroom and watch me if she chose, to see how I was doing. I must have been doing fine, since

I went to busier intersections in the following weeks. I marveled at the fact that a year ago I was living where farmers would drive their horses and wagons by the house, and we'd wave to each other. Now I was in a big city with paved streets, surrounded by bunches of cars and people, helping children often older than me, cross the street, like regular policemen I had seen in the magazines. I was so very proud of my job and my duties.

Every week I was assigned a street corner, in the mornings and the afternoons, before and after school, to let the children cross only when the street was clear. I took the belt home every night, and on the weekends I washed and scrubbed it with a stiff brush to keep it sparkling white like all patrol officers did. Or maybe their mothers did theirs. My mother didn't do mine.

In the spring, we marched in the National School Safety Patrol Parade on Constitution Ave near the Capitol. I was very proud of being in the parade. At the end of the school year I received a certificate detailing my participation in the School Safety program, sponsored by AAA. Jim tore it up to retaliate for some injustice I had done to him. I forgave him a few years later.

At first, I wasn't afraid of people. There were laws that people observed, and I never worried about my safety. Bernie fixed that.

I was on school patrol duty one morning at the intersection of a couple of quiet streets, outside a little corner market, when Bernie, a big kid, maybe thirteen years old, came by with a friend of his. I knew Bernie since I had met him with Jimmy, a neighbor's son, who was an acquaintance of mine, but Jimmy and Bernie went to Edmond Elementary.

Bernie and his friend said "Hi," to me and slid behind a small bakery truck, when the driver was inside delivering baked goods to the store. Quickly, Bernie opened the rear door of the truck, and nabbed a boxed cake as the driver ran out the door yelling,

"Stop! Stop!"

Bernie and his buddy ran parallel to each other down the street in the opposite direction from the way the truck was pointed. As the driver ran after the boy with the cake, he threw it to the other boy, and being young they outran the driver. He came panting back to me.

"Do you know the names of those punks?"

"No sir," I actually didn't know the name of the other guy, and since neither one of them went to my school, I figured I was only partly lying. I never knew Bernie's last name, anyway. The next day or so, Bernie found me walking to school, grabbed my arm in his tight fist, punched me hard in the stomach with his other hand, and asked,

"You didn't tell that guy who I was, did you?"

"No, Bernie, I didn't."

"Well, you'd better not." he said, flinging my arm, as he released it.

Jimmy had a route delivering a shopping guide in his big wooden wagon every week. The following week I was out with him one afternoon, when Bernie saw us and came over.

"Get in the wagon, a**hole," Bernie growled, giving me an evil look.

I got in the wagon. Bernie pulled me along the edge of the street as a streetcar came along and got close to us. The operator clanged his bell as Bernie pulled me onto the tracks and ran away. The streetcar stopped five or six feet away from me as I hustled out and pulled the wagon off the tracks. Maybe Bernie wasn't trying to kill me, but he sure was successful in scaring me. I didn't wet my pants, but for days, I kept scanning the streets to avoid meeting him as I walked to and from school. I never saw him again. Maybe he got locked up.

Dad bought an unseen building lot, just off of the ocean, at the beach in Assateague, Maryland, and he and Mom wanted to go see it. Early one Saturday morning, we all piled into the Nash and he drove into downtown Annapolis, where we would take the ferry across the Chesapeake Bay. The Bay Bridge wouldn't be finished until 1952. Dad filled the car with gas at the big circular Amoco service station on Main Street at the city dock, because we were going across the bay to the unknown wilderness called the Eastern Shore.

After getting gasoline, we drove onto the big ferry boat that held some sixty cars, and over a hundred people. When we left the dock, the captain announced that we could get out of our cars and walk around to see the view or visit the lounge where drinks and snacks were sold. Jim and I had fun looking at all the strange things we had never seen, like funny-looking (to us) fishing boats and seagulls that followed us.

In half an hour or so, we disembarked and drove on to Assateague. The weather was cloudy, windy, and cold, so the beach was deserted with no buildings anywhere. Dad had a plot plan with the location, but there was very little to judge where our lot was, so he and Mom estimated where the streets would be and where our lot would be.. Jim and I dug in the wet sand, and I gathered some seashells, including a nice pink conch shell, like the one Uncle Buddy had sent to my grandmother. I put several assorted oyster and clam shells in my pockets, although then I didn't know what they were, and I doubt if my parents knew. They were both mountain people. I never washed or cleaned the conch shell, and after a week, the odor was terrible, after the conch died inside the shell. Mother threw all of the shells away. I missed the conch, but the terrible stink was gone.

There was no one else at the beach, and because it was cold and windy, we were happy to get back into the car and return home, taking the big ferry boat back across the Bay. It had been a long and exhausting day, but we had learned about the Eastern Shore, and the ocean. Later, Dad received a notice that the government was buying all the lots at Assateague for a National Park. He had paid $395 for the lot. He received $3,900 from the federal government, but the family dream was gone.

We weren't Catholic, but every Friday, Lent, or not, Mother always served fish for dinner. Usually it was salmon cakes or tuna casserole. On Fridays I always wanted to be anywhere except sitting in DC trying to eat salmon cakes or tuna casserole. I felt I was eating "Puss and Boots," salmon, because I found an occasional bone in the canned salmon. It wasn't cat food, but I knew it wasn't one of the more expensive brands of canned salmon, because I bought it. Problem was, Mother wasn't a great cook. It seemed we ate salmon cakes burned in lard every other week. Sometimes it would be filet of fish. I'd eat that, just for the halibut. Oops, Sorry.

Since then, I've come to love salmon. Just not the way

Mom cooked it.

I could eat tuna salad because I could concentrate on the mayonnaise and the little chunks of celery and onion, but the tuna casserole didn't offer me any good options, so I spread the tuna mixture around on my plate, hoping the plate would absorb some. But even if it didn't, the plate looked like I had eaten more than I had. Jim had a major, major problem with eating boiled or creamed spinach. He would sit there with an anguished look on his face and pout. Once he dropped some on the floor, and Mom grabbed him around the neck, pulled him off his chair, and yelled in her "sailor" language as she rubbed his nose in it on the floor. While Mom fought with us about eating these foods, Dad stayed silent, and ate whatever Mom served us, so I never knew whose side he was on.

I never had eaten spaghetti until I moved to DC, even though Mother had tried to get me to eat it in West Virginia. Mom made Chef Boyardee spaghetti for dinner about once a week. It came in a box with all the ingredients, including a little can of parmesan cheese and a can of sauce in the same box. It wasn't great, but it wasn't salmon.The milkman brought a couple of quarts of milk in glass bottles twice a week. The night before he delivered, it was my job to put the glass bottles out to be returned, for re-use. Sometime during this period we stopped getting milk delivered, and with Mom's instructions, I bought powdered milk and I learned to make our milk in a pitcher. It tasted like talcum-powdered water. Mom had me buy Velveeta Cheese, and for lunch we might have a grilled Velveeta Cheese sandwich and tomato soup. That was my introduction to cheese, and it became my favorite meal.

As I said, we weren't Catholic. Mom and Dad never

went to church, but Mom took me down the street and around to the big Presbyterian Church at the corner of 9th and Maryland Ave and enrolled me in Sunday School. I was in a small class consisting of Simon, who was the minister's son, and me. Again, like third grade, I was half of the entire class. Our teacher, Ms. Harris, the church secretary, was a very nice lady who would give us an assignment and leave us alone. BTW, "Ms." didn't exist then. It hadn't been coined or defined as a woman who could or could not be a Miss or Mrs. I'm not sure, but I'm thinking I called her Miss Harris. Simon always talked fast. He said to me the first day I met him, as part of his introduction to me,

"I can recite all the books in the Bible in less than a minute. Want a' hear?"

I had gotten an Elgin wristwatch on my first Christmas in DC and I had worn it to Sunday School. When Simon saw it he asked me to time him to show me how quickly he could say all the books. He was about a minute, I suppose, but he sounded like the voices reading the fine print on those radio ads. Plus, as far as I knew, he could have skipped fifteen of them. I knew Genesis and Exodus in the Old Testament, and Matthew, Mark. Luke, and John, in the New Testament, from Mom's old Bible where Richard Allen Black's card was kept. I didn't know all the books in the Bible then, nor now, but Simon (who knew a lot about Christian religion) and Ms. Harris taught me a lot. I used that knowledge through the years including when I became the Superintendent of Sunday School, in a church I joined after I was married.

I mentioned my Elgin watch. My watch was magnificent. It had a metal expandable band, and I loved it for years. Alas, I ruined the watch by plunging it into a barrel of pickles when I worked for Marriott. Later in life, I would work in Elgin, IL, and use some of the Elgin Watch Company's furniture that my employer had bought from the sale after the watch company had closed. Funny how the world turns.

On November 20,1949, Mom was admitted to Children's Hospital. After Baby Jan came the next day, which was Thanksgiving, Dad took Jim and me downtown and had us wait on the sidewalk, while he went in to visit Mom. No children under twelve were allowed to visit in the maternity ward, even after the babies were born. No Dads were allowed in the delivery room then or later, even when my children were born. I had watched calves being born, so I knew how birthing worked anyway, so that wasn't a problem. In a few minutes we could see Mother inside the window on the fourth floor, waving to us. When Dad came back down, he took us to a Hot Shoppes cafeteria nearby for lunch. Jim and I had turkey. Jan had milk, I guess. It was my first time eating turkey, and my first visit to Hot Shoppes Restaurants, a restaurant chain owned by J.W. Marriott, who didn't have any hotels then, only restaurants. I would work for him and learn about the formal and informal rules of employment. I'll tell you about that later.

I was ten the next school year when I walked alone six blocks to seventh grade in Stuart Junior High School, at 5th and "E", now Stuart-Hobson Middle School, and Jim went to Edmund, the elementary school a block away. None of my friends at Maury went to Stuart, since it was not the Junior High School those children attended, so it was new school, number six for me, and I had to make new friends, except for Jimmy, who was a year ahead of me. At Stuart, not only did we have formal art classes, but we had music, and physical education, too. I'd never had any of those as classes. Thankfully I didn't see Bernie.

After I decided that the trombone was the instrument I wanted to play, Mom and Dad took me to a music store and bought me a shiny, new Conn trombone. I took lessons and practiced at home which helped me develop the "lip" necessary to play. My apologies to those who suffered from my practicing. Band class was one day a week, and we played only in class. I never became really proficient, but I learned to read music, and I played the trombone through high school. In music class we sang songs that were popular then, like ***Mona Lisa,*** by Nat King Cole, and ***Harbor Lights***, which was an old hit that became popular again in 1950 with Sammy Kaye and his orchestra.

On Halloween, the school held a party out back on the playground. We came to school in our costumes. I was the Devil. My two-doors-up neighbor, Sue, was an angel. We played a game as partners with a group. Then when it was over we drifted off and talked. When the music started, she grabbed my hand and we awkwardly danced. She was cute. I could tell there were no cooties on her. My insides fluttered. Her mother picked her up after the party, and I shuffled home with that strange feeling in my stomach. I don't remember ever having even another conversation with her, but I probably did at school. At home, if I saw her outside, I would wave. The families weren't friends. Our parents would wave and call "Hello," or something when we saw each other outside, but we never had any conversation with any of the neighbors, except Mom's friends, which I will talk about in a minute, and of course, Karen. Dad was not a sociable guy at home. I'm guessing he was much more sociable at work.

I joined the Boy Scouts and became a Tenderfoot. I remember the uniform, the badge, and going to the meetings. I remember riding with a bunch of boys in the Scoutmaster's '49 Nash, the monster car that looked like an upside-down bathtub, but I don't remember us doing any camping.

There were classes we could choose that only met on Friday afternoons for four weeks. I took a class in printing for boys only. We used the California Case, part of a system of typesetting that was common then in letterpress printing. Every typesetter had a large wooden box, about three feet by two feet that was placed tilted on a riser, for easy picking. The typesetter sat on a stool to easily reach all of the boxes. The box had maybe two hundred small various-sized compartments in it that held thin removable pieces of steel about one inch long, ⅜" wide, with various thicknesses. Each piece had one letter, number or punctuation embossed on one end. Each of us had to set the type for a sentence or two by picking out each letter, number, or punctuation mark from the little compartment where it was stored, and placing it in a tool called a composing stick that we held. This tool would very tightly handle up to six lines of type, then a pressman would secure it in a large form that held a lot of composing stick units to print a page in the newspaper. All we had to do was handset a sentence and print it on a piece of paper. In four weeks we finished that project. Thankfully that system is gone now with offset and digital printing.

I took a boy's home economics class every Friday for a month. The only thing we learned to do was to make cinnamon toast. We had to butter the toast, mix the cinnamon and brown sugar, and sprinkle the mixture on the bread. Being the smart seventh-grade boys that we were, we learned how to do that in four weeks, too.

My first paid babysitting job was with Mom's friend, Elisabeth. Her daughter, Cheryl, was probably six or seven months old the first time I baby sat when the moms went out. By keeping Jan, I knew how to deal with babies, feeding from a bottle, and changing cloth diapers. No disposable diapers then. I was ten, but I felt grown up and proud to have the responsibility. I don't remember how much I got paid, but I was thrilled to do it.

Mom's other close friend, Anne, didn't have children, but she was married to a musician who played the trombone. Is that where I got the idea to play the trombone? Probably. Anne would come down in the evening from her apartment up the street, with a bottle of Petre wine when Mom invited her, and the two women would sit at the table in the kitchen/dining area, sipping the wine, smoking their cigarettes, and solving the problems of the world as it pertained to them and their two families.

Somewhere in this time frame, Grandad and Grandmom came to Washington to visit. Dad went to Union Station and picked them up. I had lived in DC long enough that I saw how out of date they were. Their clothes, for one thing, although Grandma wore dresses that she had ordered from the Montgomery Ward catalogue. The couple looked old and tired, but Grandad was cheerful and pleasant. Grandma was quiet, as she always was around people she didn't know well. Looking back, after I left West Virginia, I don't remember Mother ever going back to Leander to visit after I left. I went back once, I'll talk about that later, but Grandma's visit to us must have been a strain on both women. I don't remember the two of them being friendly, or not friendly, just two people who didn't pay attention to each other. When we went to

Ohio for Dad's reunions, we never came close to Leander.

I was shocked at the difference in their dialect, since I hadn't heard anyone speak in the distinct mountain voice that I had used just a year or so before. Remember, when I lived In West Virginia, there was no national TV that over a few years would standardize dialects all over the country, to a very large extent. It and my surroundings had quickly changed mine to a great extent. There are still differences, but today's dialects aren't nearly as diversified as they were before nationwide TV.

This time I knew and appreciated the beauty of the city when I went with them as Dad showed them the sights of DC. After a couple of days Dad took them back to the train. I cried when they left. Seeing them had brought back the memories of my old life. I was becoming happy here. I missed the country life, but I knew that part of my life was over. I was in DC to stay. What, Mark? "**It's what you know for sure that just ain't so.**"

After Jan was six months old, Mom got a part-time night hostess's job at the Mayflower Hotel in their very classy restaurant. When she went to work, she would fix her hair, put on her makeup, a white blouse, dark blue skirt, and high heels, and ride the streetcar downtown to her job on Connecticut Avenue, NW. She was a beautiful 37-year-old woman, with a look of sophistication that hid her background of being a country girl. Or, maybe not. I was too young to tell, but to me, she looked beautiful.

The Mayflower Hotel was (and still is) a five star hotel where the A-list people met, (and still do) including piano-player and songwriter, Hoagy Carmichael, who wrote over 100 songs, with fifty of them being hit records, including ***Stardust,*** and ***Georgia on my Mind.*** In those days, Hoagy

Carmichael was what Taylor Swift is today, a writer and performer that captures the headlines wherever she goes. I will say, he wasn't nearly as sexy as she is, but that's my personal opinion. The point is they both were extremely talented professionals.

Every night Mom met the national celebrities and internationally known people who came to the Mayflower, including Drew Pearson, who then worked for the Washington Post. His news and opinions were syndicated in 500 newspapers and radio stations all over the U.S. and Europe. Drew Pearson had been all over the world, and every day since the 1930's he had used his typewriter for what he thought was important for Americans to know. As I said, his column The Washington-Merry-Go-Round was in the Charleston Gazette that Grandad read daily,We did not have CNN or Fox News, nor any of the computerized news agencies we have today, so when the Korean war started Pearson was in high demand by papers and radio stations all over the world, for what was happening in DC.

When Mr. Pearson came to the Mayflower to meet and talk to dignitaries who were staying there, he would tip Mom with a twenty dollar bill. A twenty-dollar tip bought us two weeks of groceries for our family in 1950. Looking back, I'm sure she enjoyed working there among the famous and moneyed people. I don't remember names other than those two, but I know there were plenty more because it was a happening place.

How did Dad feel about all this? I don't know, but I do know that somewhere around this time, Dad decided he wanted to be a Gentleman Farmer. Why? I'm not sure. Maybe it was because Mom was really zoning in on her job. Maybe there was something more nefarious going on. Maybe it was because of Karen and me. Maybe he just wanted fresh tomatoes. Maybe it was all of that, and more, but I think I can say with certainty that it wasn't my mother's idea.

From that time on, every Sunday morning, Dad would load the family in the Nash and we would go out of the city to look for a farm to buy. We looked and looked. North, South, and West. Not much East because of the Chesapeake Bay.

Finally, Dad found a farm on the County line between Spotsylvania and Orange Counties in Virginia, near Paytes, Va. It had about two hundred acres of rolling hills, with eighty acres cleared and 120 acres of woodland. To get to it, you turned off of Tatum Road near where it intersects with St. Just Rd, both gravel roads then, onto a private road down a mile of dusty and, in one place, a very muddy road. The road does not exist today.

Dad bought the property for $8,000, about $40 an acre. He sold our house to Karen's family.

There was really no farming happening on the farm that Dad bought. There was an older tenant (or maybe he was a squatter) with a French accent living there with his wife, who had a few chickens that shared the two-story farmhouse with them. When the tenant opened the door the first time to greet us, a chicken came with him from inside the house to see who we were. Mom told me to stay outside and watch Jim and Jan while they went in. I was happy to stay out, since having chickens running around inside your house usually means you have a messy floor.

My screwed-up life was about to be screwed up again, but this time Mom's life would be screwed up too. **"What doesn't kill us makes us stronger, "** said everyone.

Part Three

VIRGINIA Don't forget, living in DC, our Mom was an attractive 37-year-old woman who had worked her way up from living in a place with no electricity around anywhere, to being a hostess at one of the finest hotels in the United States, where she met the world leaders and celebrities who came to DC, the capital of the greatest country in the world, after WWII. It was a long, long, long way from living in Leander.

I remind you of this again because I want you to remember it, as I tell you about our living through the next five years.

Dad had grown up in the little town of Hamlin WV, population 200 people, isolated in the hills of West Virginia, where his father owned a general store. But, as I said, for some unknown, but probable, reasons, Dad decided he wanted to become a Gentleman Farmer. A Gentleman Farmer is the farmer who sits on the front porch in the evening, drinking sweet tea, and looking out over his pasture at the herd of cattle that he doesn't milk, but lets them get fat as they graze on lush green grass, like the farmer that Tennesse Williams wrote about; the father who was played by Berl Ives in the movie, ***Cat on a Hot Tin Roof.*** He had a son, a former local football hero, played by Paul Newman, who was married to a beautiful woman, played by Elizabeth Taylor. Even if you saw the movie, see the movie trailer on Wikipedia, Certainly see it, if you don't know what I'm talking about. It's riveting. Warning, It'll make you want to see the movie. Again.

Mother had grown up with her parents, where I lived for

nine years while Mother and Dad got their lives together. The family had hand-milked the cows, plowed the fields with a horse, raised hogs and chickens, grew their own food and sold the surplus if there was any. They knew about calluses on their hands from hoeing the weeds out of the corn, and back-aches from stooping over rows of vegetables while harvesting them. As a preteen, I didn't know it then, but my mother wasn't happy about becoming the wife of a farmer.

The rear part of the house in Virginia had been built before the Civil War. The front part of the house was built around 1900, and originally had gas lights in it, with the old light fixtures still mounted on the walls. The acetylene gas had been made in another building that had been torn or burned down, but the old tank that held the calcium carbide pellets and some of the equipment was laying on the ground near where the building had been. To make the acetylene gas, water was dripped on the pellets and the resulting gas was piped into the house to the gas lights. It produced a nice light when it burned, and was a fairly common way for well-to-do people to have lights before electricity was available. Towns and cities often used this method to produce gas lights on the streets until electricity became available. Acetylene gas is sold in tanks now and used in welding shops.

The tenant (squatter?) grew some scruffy-looking corn on a tiny part of the red clay land that was close to the house,and had been over-farmed. The other fields were full of broom sage grass and trees that had sprung up along the neglected fence lines where the birds sat after eating the seeds of the trees and had unknowingly planted the trees.

As part of the property transaction, there was a 1946

civilian, faded green Jeep, with no cab or canopy, a two-horse-drawn mowing machine, and an old, two-horse farm wagon that had large wooden-spoke wheels. Buildings other than the house consisted of an old barn in major decline, a two-room corn crib, a smokehouse built out of logs with a dirt floor, and a log cabin that had been lived in by the slaves. Both of the log structures were built over a hundred years before. There was no chicken house. Nothing on the property was in good condition. Electricity was not available, so no running water, no central heat, only two tin heaters in two downstairs rooms. Only one disintegrating fireplace in the old part of the house that was too dangerous to use. Mom had already lived that way, she didn't want to go back. Jim and I were excited, but I know now, Mom was not.

The way the property looked, and what Mom must have been thinking, really the whole thing, makes me think of Scarlett O'Hara, miserable, but determined in ***Gone With The Wind***, when she says to herself,

"I'll think about that tomorrow."

Mom and Dad closed on the property and the tenant moved on to his next adventure, taking his wife and chickens. There were no animals on the farm when we closed. I never saw any animals other than the chickens in the house and a dog. There was no chicken house. Dad had a sign made with decorative black lettering on white that said:

DEEP-IN-WOODS

FARM

JENNINGS ROBERTS

He planted the 30 by 18 inch sign close to the county's gravel road where our private, mile-long dirt, and muddy road began alongside a neighbor's small field, on one side with woods on the other side. Then the road went through the woods until it came to our farm, a mile away, Deep In the Woods.

Dad bought a hundred-pound bag of dried pinto beans for less than four dollars, and warned us that beans and tomatoes would be the main items in our diet until the mortgage was paid off. I was OK with that, since I had eaten a lot of dried beans living with my grandparents in West Virginia, but my young sister, Jan, wasn't. She still doesn't like them. For the next three years we would buy cases of canned tomatoes in the winter and spring and grow tomatoes and other vegetables in our garden during the summer and fall. It was a life that consumed Mom.

I must admit, Dad worked hard to build the farm and made Jim and me work hard for our young ages, which of course, was super good training, although It made me decide to never remodel a house..

Because we still lived in Washington, Dad, Jim, and I, and sometimes Mom and Jan, came down every weekend to rescue the house. The slave quarters' cabin built with logs before the Civil War was in better shape than the house, so we tried to close up the holes between the logs with cement so we could live in it on the weekends. The windows in the log cabin did not have glass. We boarded them up, but the wind still came through all the places that we couldn't close up with cement.When it was cold that winter, we built a fire in the old stone fireplace, but it was still cold. Spending the nights with goosebumps was standard procedure. For those trips, we had canned corn beef sandwiches with mustard or Spam sandwiches on a good day. Dad had ordered electricity, but the Electric Co-op Company had to clear a right-of-way about a half mile through the woods for the power lines.

Dad personally wired the house for electricity and put in plumbing and a bathroom in the house. I don't know where he learned those trades, but he was pretty good at it. One Saturday, when it was just him and me, we left the Nash at the farm, and we took the Jeep up Rt 1, and got on the Shirley Highway, now I-395. In those days it was one lane in each direction from Lorton to just south of Shirlington. That evening he went to Sears and came home with a bathtub that stuck out on the tailgate of the Jeep.

Sunday morning, he and I went back to the farm. By then Dad had put an aluminum top on the Jeep, but it was still a cold trip that day with no heater in the Jeep and the rear open with the bathtub hanging out.

We stopped in at the old Falmouth diner on Rt. 1 near Fredericksburg, for breakfast when I asked,

"Dad, who is going to help us carry that tub up the stairs?"

He simply said, "I don't have anybody. We'll see."

I spent the rest of the trip trying to conjure up ways the two of us could get it up stairs. I came to the conclusion that there was no way we could do it.

When we got to the house he backed the Jeep across the yard up to the front door. There was no front porch. Just inside the open door, the stairs seemed to laugh at me. I don't know if they laughed at Dad. He took the step ladder upstairs and climbed up the ladder with a hatchet in his hand, and in line with the stairs that went straight down to the front door, he chipped away the plaster and the lathes on the ceiling near the wall. Then he fastened a short piece of chain to the rafter where he had exposed it. As he was doing all of that, he asked me to go into the dining room where all of the tools were stored, and bring the block and tackle upstairs.

A block and tackle is a complicated arrangement of pulleys and ropes with hooks on both ends that when hooked up properly can be used to move a heavy object. The light went on in my head. It obviously had already been burning in his.

He hooked one end of the block and tackle to the chain around the rafter, then took the hook on the other end down and hooked it to the Jeep. He took the rope on the block and tackle and tied it to the tub through the hole for the faucet. Then he said,

"Get in the Jeep, and just barely move forward a couple of inches while I make sure everything is alright as it comes through the door,"

I got into the Jeep and moved it four or five inches. The tub came off of the Jeep and started through the door. As it came off the Jeep, Dad scooted the tub away from the wooden door frame, and shortly it was in the house. Then I would move the Jeep forward a few inches, until he would yell,

"Stop!"

It reminded me of the old game, Mother, May I? It only

took about five minutes to get the tub upstairs. When it was upstairs, we smiled at each other because it was a huge relief to both of us, and I was proud of us for getting it up the stairs. We lifted the end of the tub and set it on an old quilt and dragged it into the bathroom. A couple of banisters would need to be painted, and the exposed rafter had to be covered with drywall or plaster, but no real damage was done to anything.

There was still no electricity, but he installed an electric water pump in the large, old, four-foot diameter, hand-dug well that was lined with rocks of various sizes that had been picked up in the field by people many years ago. He wired the house for lights and outlets. In those days no one had air conditioning in their house, and very few stores were air-conditioned. It would be 30 years before electric radiant heat would be used extensively in homes, but Dad installed it in that old farmhouse. The radiant heat came from special glass panels mounted in the wall and controlled by thermostats in every room. It was the start of an industry, but I never saw those glass panels installed in any other building. There were no inspections by any authorities, because no permits had been issued. I doubt if the county even had a permitting program in place then.

While Dad worked on the plumbing and wiring, unless he needed us, Dad said for Jim and I to take up the wood flooring in the kitchen, and fill the void up with dirt. I started bringing soil through the back door to the ten-foot by ten-foot kitchen. to fill the three-foot void so that we could pour a concrete floor. I filled the wheelbarrow with dirt from the garden and pushed it up the incline into the kitchen and dumped it. It took me many weekends to fill that huge void. I was doing other things based on what

Dad wanted me to do, and I was 11, not 18.

The old chimney for the dangerous fireplace was beyond repair, so Dad tied a rope around it, and I pulled it down with the Jeep. Then Jim and I dismantled the old fireplace and chimney and stacked all of the usable bricks for future use as a back yard walkway and patio. A lot of the old bricks were crumbly, and not usable.

The walls in the house were made with plaster on lathes. Lathes are small, thin, two-inch-wide strips of wood nailed to the studs in the walls of the rooms. The walls were in very poor shape in most places. We tore down the plaster where it had cracked and pulled away from the wall, exposing the lathes, we stuffed insulation in the cavities around the studs and lathes, but we never recovered the walls, so as long as we lived there we looked at the old, crappy, brown lathes, and dark-colored insulation. While Dad worked on things that required some knowledge, Jim and I were the grunts, working together on chores that didn't require much knowledge, like painting doors, or helping Dad by holding something in place while he cut it. If we screwed up, Dad would yell at us, and then calm down, and jokingly mutter,

"I've seen better heads on nickel beers!" or "Give me that! You two look like two monkeys (making love to) a football!!"

When the buds came out in the spring, and electricity came to the house, we moved to the farm. As kids, Jim and I were excited. Mom was much less excited. Her living standard had been put back to when she was a child in West Virginia. This time she had no kitchen, or hot water. This time she did have electricity and a cold-water bathroom, but this time she also had a young toddler who could walk, a second grader with dirty hands, and an eleven year old who was starting to become a teenager. She had no phone; heating water was a chore, and the closest neighbors were more than a mile away up our dusty, and muddy road.

We had put gravel on top of my fill dirt, but no concrete yet, so Dad bought a cast-iron, flat-topped, wood-burning cook stove that he put in the dining room and knocked a hole in the wall to install the smoke pipe so we could cook and have hot water. We heated our water in a large fifteen gallon steel wash tub on the flat-topped wood stove, (Just like two hundred years ago, right?)

One Sunday while Dad, Jim, and I were trimming apple trees nearby in the orchard, we heard Mom screaming. We went running to the house, jumping over the strand of barbed wire fence that we had installed over the row of multiflora rose bushes that separated the yard from the Orchard.

A cast-iron stove leg had broken in half, causing the door to the fire box to come open, and had flung fire and hot coals on the wood floor in the dining room. The tilted stove also dumped the hot water from the tub on the fire, so when we got there, there was no fire, but a lot of steam, smoke and a big mess, with a burned wood floor, but no injuries. No hits, no runs, maybe an error.

But it was a major strike against the farm in Mom's mind.

For a couple of weeks, Dad took me back to DC to Stuart Jr. High, but neither of us enjoyed that, since it took him out of his way to deliver me to the school, and I had to endure an hour and a half of intense inspection and interrogation of my actions and behavior by an attorney, who just happened to be my Dad. The questions and instructions about life in general, and my life in particular, flew from his mouth like hornets from a nest. I swatted the questions with answers, but I still got stung a lot. I had been used to picking on my brother on the way to school, but in this situation I was no longer Alpha Dog.

I don't remember any of the questions, but I remember the dread in my body when I got in the car, both in the morning and the trip home. Sometimes he lectured me on the law, and national politics. One morning he said,

"Tomorrow morning, I want you to recite the opening paragraph of the Declaration of Independence to me from memory."

He reached into his suit coat pocket and handed me a paper with the Declaration of Independence printed on it.

"Read the whole thing to me now." I read it to him.

"Now you can just learn the first paragraph for tomorrow."

In my mind, to myself, not outloud, "Why is he doing this? I'll never use this. He's just torturing me." But I did it.

"When in the course of human events, it becomes necessary for one people to dissolve the political bands which have connected them with another, and to assume among the powers of the earth the separate and equal nation to which the powers of the earth,,,," yada, yada, yada. I realize now, all of that was for my own good. Five years later, I realized I could dissolve all of my physical bands and most of the emotional bands, from my people too, so:

"Dad, thanks for that."

The old Nash always smelled of cigar smoke. He smoked one going to work in the morning, and another on the way home. To tell the truth, I got used to it and I enjoyed that part of the trip. Somewhere in that time, since Dad drove over 160 miles every day, he traded in the '47 Nash and bought a new 1952 Nash Rambler from Nash-Kelvinator Co. I mention their full name because Kelvinator had merged with Nash and still made refrigerators. The '52 Rambler was about the size of a big refrigerator, as it seemed to be just slightly bigger than the Nash Metropolitan, which was made in England, and sold here. As I said, the large '49 Nash sedan looked like an upside-down bathtub.

After two weeks my travel arrangement with Dad was vetoed by both Dad and me, so Mom enrolled me in the seventh grade at the Unionville Elementary School. As it was my sixth different school, that meant I had to start over with new friends, but in my mind that was better than what I was going through riding for two hours with Dad. These friends would last me forever. What? **"It ain't what you don't know that gets you into trouble. It's what you know for sure that just ain't so."**

Every morning Mom and Jan would take Jim and me up our private road in the Jeep to catch the old, yellow, wooden, Ford school bus for the 15 mile ride to school. In the afternoons we walked the mile home from the bus. In 1951, I was in the seventh grade at Unionville, where the school broadcast General MacArthur's speech over the PA system when he spoke to Congress and famously said,

"Old soldiers never die. They just fade away."

MacArthur, a General with a big ego, had grown a bigger ego since he had defeated the Japanese six or seven years earlier. And had recently disturbed President Truman, who fired him when he did not stop invading North Korea as Truman had wanted him to do. Like a lot of Presidents, Truman fired people who didn't do what they were told to do.

Mr. Banks, our good-humored, young teacher, came up with a fun project. Every week when he had an hour of us singing in what was an informal music class, he taught us to sing an old song from World War One, called Reuben, Reuben, that went like this:

"Ruben, Ruben, I've been thinking,

What a great world this would be,

If the men were all transported

Far beyond the Northern Sea!

Rachel, Rachel, I've been thinking,

What a good world this would be,

If the girls were all transported

Far beyond the Northern Sea."

It was a snappy little tune, and everyone enjoyed singing it, but, after I arrived, since there was a "Richard" and a "Rachel" in the class, Mr. Banks had us change the words to "Richard and Rachel." To the delight of everyone else, Rachel, a freckled redhead, and I, both blushed every time the song was sung.

One of my friends was Billy Anderson (Not his real name). Billy's personal hygiene left a lot to be desired, but he and I were friends. Mother was at the school one day and I introduced her to Billy. I guess she really surveyed him, because later, when she was driving me wherever we were going, she started in on me about him. She said his teeth had crud on them, because he hadn't brushed them for weeks. His face was dirty, his hair was messy, and his clothes were dirty. "I don't want you going to school looking like that," she said. I knew all that, but she used Billy's appearance to reinforce cleaner standards on me. When I missed something, she always said, "You look like Billy." When my appearance looked good, I got a "Hot spit. You look nice."

I told you about my grandmother doing the laundry in West Virginia. Doing laundry now was almost as hard. Dad wore a suit and tie to work. The only things that went to the cleaners were Dad's suits. That meant five white shirts washed and ironed at the house every week. Mom had a child in diapers. There were two boys who got clothes dirty just standing still. Mom had hot water now, and a washing machine with a wringer, but no dryer. Everything had to be hung outside, except in rainy weather, when she used three racks that she loaded with clothes and dried in the house. She taught me how to wash and fold clothes, and she bought metal pants stretchers that we put in the blue jeans, which everyone except Jan wore, after washing so they dried straight. I sat the ironing board up in the dining room, and through the weeks I learned how to iron Dad's dress shirts, but I tried to avoid that job, since it was fussy work. I ironed a lot of things like handkerchiefs, and some of Jim and my shirts and Mom's blouses when they came through the wash.

Because in those days there weren't any professors who knew aeronautical law, Dad wound up teaching Aeronautical Law at Georgetown on Saturday mornings for a while. One Saturday, with Dad in DC, 80 miles away, Mom got a second strike when the field behind the house caught on fire. Mom had started the fire to burn something, maybe some trash, but the fire spread, burning the field behind the house, and got out of control. Because there was still no phone, she sent me to get a neighbor or anyone to come help fight it. Barefoot, wearing shorts with no shirt, and my heart in my throat, I jumped in the Jeep, and drove to find someone to help. After three or four miles of not finding anyone home, I found an old man who was mowing weeds along the road. I asked him to help, and he climbed in the Jeep.

I was driving fast down the county's gravel road, when the old man asked with tension in his voice,

"How old are you?"

"Twelve," I lied. (I was still eleven)

"Well, you sure can drive,"

By the time we got to the house, Mom had managed to get the fire under control. She drove the old man back to where he had been working.

Dad had cut the long two-horse tongue off of the mower, so we could pull it with the Jeep. Early Saturday mornings, for a few hours, Dad would sit on the mower, while I drove the Jeep, and as he mowed, he would yell, "Gee," or "Haw," the words a farmer would give to his team of horses that pulled the mower, to make them go right or left. In addition, Dad gave me other instructions, such as telling me to take the mower along our driveway. Driving the Jeep was the best part of living there for me, even though he often fussed at me.

After we finished mowing or doing something else around the farm, later in the morning, we would all get in the car and go to Orange to shop at the Safeway grocery store, go to the bank, and perhaps the hardware store. Looking back I can see what a motley crew we must have been. Now, Mom's dress-up clothes were mostly clean wrap-around denim skirts. Jan would point and babble as she stood in the grocery cart or as I carried her. No child seats in grocery carts then. Jim and I would follow Mom around talking or pleading with her for whatever we saw and thought would be good to eat or be fun to have. It seldom worked.

Mom always bought a five pound package of hamburger and a box of Velveeta Cheese, if we were out of Velveeta. When we got home, she cooked cheeseburgers for a late lunch. Sunday mornings, we might have chipped beef and gravy on Pillsbury biscuits for breakfast, or fried apples from the orchard in season. Other times the menu might be fried eggs and bacon. When school was in session, during the week, I would usually make oatmeal with powdered milk for the three of us. The powdered milk still tasted like talcum water. Sometimes on Saturday nights, Mom would ask me if I wanted to make some fudge. I always did. I cooked the cocoa, sugar, a touch of vanilla extract, and powdered milk, and checked the doneness by dripping a spoonful on a saucer of water, and rolling it in my fingers. If it rolled nicely into a ball, I took it off the stove and poured it on wax paper. I waited five minutes for it to cool and harden then cut it into squares. Yummy! If there was snow outside, I would take a clean pot and fill it with snow, bring it inside and add sugar, a small amount of vanilla, and just a bit of powdered milk, stir it up and serve everyone ice cream.

For dinner, we ate a lot of dried pinto beans and tomatoes along with an occasional boiled chicken.

Yes, I said "boiled." Poached, if you insist. It was seldom fried and never baked.

In season we had food from the garden, including cabbage, potatoes, fresh tomatoes, green beans, corn, cucumbers, watermelon, cantaloupe, and.... strawberries.

We had set out two long rows of strawberry plants immediately after we bought the farm, before we even moved in. By doing some hand trimming of unwanted shoots, by the second year, we were swimming in strawberries. Every day during their season we would pick strawberries and eat them, or give them away to Mom's friend, Oma Lena, or A.C. Hazelgrove and his wife, Irene.

If the strawberries were starting to rot, or were not fit to keep, Jim and I would throw them at each other, as we did with the tomatoes later in the season. Strawberries could sting. Rotten tomatoes stank, and were messy so after the pond was built, we would jump in the pond to swim the odor and pieces of the tomatoes off our clothes and bodies. Sometimes he and I stripped and just skinny-dipped.

A.C. and Irene Hazelgrove were the couple who lived in

the rear of the general store that they owned and also served as the postmaster for the community of Granite Springs, VA, which was our simple address. Every day or so, when school was out, Mom would take us to go get the mail or buy something she needed. Their store probably had it, but it was expensive to buy big things from them.

One day when we went in the store, A.C., a heavy man, was standing at the main counter with his glasses propped on his forehead,(as they always seemed to be), eating some strange sloppy-looking things sitting on a newspaper, using his pocket knife as a fork. Mother asked him,

"What's that?"

"Mountain Oysters." Puzzled, Mother asked, *"What's that*?"

"Calf testicles."

Mom blanched and replied,

"Oh!" she shuddered, and moved on deeper into the store.

Jan loved the Jeep. By the time she was two, if we mentioned it, she would get excited and point toward the parking lot and say,

"Yeep, Yeep."

To avoid saying Jeep and other words that set her off, we started speaking in Pig Latin, when talking about something we wanted to hide from her. For those of you who don't know about Pig Latin, it is simply taking the sound of the first letter off the word and putting it on the end of the word adding a long A. So Jeep becomes "eepJA."

"et'sLA oG*A* oTA eTA oreStA. etGA nIA heTA eepJA," translated is:

"Let's go to the store. Get in the Jeep." or close to it.

In six weeks she had learned Pig Latin and was speaking it. When Jan was around this age, if Mom was fussing about something, or about to tell us to do or stop doing something, we would get Jan to run through the house, yelling,

"Look out boy's, Momma's on the warpath."

Sometimes it would work, and Mom would laugh. Sometimes it wouldn't work, but we three loved to do it.

Living in DC we had the advantage of having television. It was not a given because now we lived eighty miles away. Dad was a big Redskins fan, and Charlie "Choo Choo" Justice was a big-star running back for the Redskins. There was even a song about him, "***All the way, Choo Choo***." The whole question of TV on the farm seemed to hang on getting to see Charlie play. Usually, the home games of the Washington Redskins were televised from Richmond, not Washington, because there was a NFL rule that if the local stadium did not sell out for a game the game couldn't be televised locally. That meant Dad never saw the home games when we lived in DC. Here, the antenna would face Washington with their four channels during the week and when Washington played at home on Sundays, the antenna needed to be turned so it would be facing Richmond, because the home games of the Redskins seldom sold out in those days.

We didn't know if we could have TV reception from Richmond, but neighbors had TV from DC, so we cut down a tree, cut off a twenty foot log, and trimmed the branches off. Jim and I peeled the bark off the pole and painted it with caustic creosote, a dark thin liquid that is used to treat railroad ties. Creosote burns your skin and hurts if you get it on your arm or leg. Of course Jim and I got it on our skin a lot.

With Dad's instructions and help, using large U-bolts, we loosely fastened a twenty-foot length of 1-1/4 inch steel pipe to the top of the pole. We screwed a large bolt through the wood below the pipe to keep the pipe from sliding down the pole. That way, the pipe could be turned with a large pipe wrench. On the top of the pipe, we attached a five-foot TV antenna with cable.

Then, using a hand-held post hole digger, we dug a hole in the ground several feet away from the house. With the help of the tractor, we put the twenty-foot tree with the twenty-foot pipe and five foot antenna in the ground and tamped the dirt securely around it. We ran the line from the antenna to the living room window and into the house to the TV. It worked, but not great. Not like living in the city.

To change reception to Richmond on home-game Sundays, Dad or I put an extension ladder against the pole and climbed up with a big pipe wrench and turned the pipe, while someone in the living room, yelled,

"More, a little more," or

"Back a little, more, more." and then,

"Hold it!,"

The person inside, looking at the TV screen, yelled the messages to someone outside, who yelled commands to the person on the pole, until the antenna was situated in the right spot toward Richmond. After the football game, we reversed the entire procedure and turned the antenna back toward DC for the rest of the week. Problem solved, but the picture always looked like it was snowing either way it was facing, because we were so far away from the transmitters. I remember seeing the Coronation of Queen Elizabeth in England one Saturday in November 1952 through the ever-present snow on the screen.

In 1953, along with 80 million other people, I watched some of the McCarthy hearings. Joseph McCarthy, a Senator from Wisconsin, was chairman of a Subcommittee that he used as a platform to try to prove there were Communists in the State Department, and elsewhere in the US Government. For his legal team, he chose Roy Cohn as chief counsel. Cohn would later become the attorney for Donald Trump and his father. Cohn supposedly taught Donald that people would believe lies if you told the same lie long enough. Donald is rumored as saying he missed having Cohn around. The assistant chief counsel was Robert F. Kennedy, the father of RFK,Jr, the Secretary of Health and Human Services under President Trump. McCarthy was censured by the Senate later that year after being discredited.

Dad's sister, Shirley, was a close friend of Mom's, and my favorite aunt of the six that I had, because she was funny, and she accepted me as an adult. She came from Ohio to visit us at some point. She didn't bring her two children or husband with her, so it was just two forty-year-old girls, with Jim, Jan, and me tagging along when the two adventurous women decided to drive four hours each way to Virginia Beach for the day, Shirley had her '48 Chevy. Mother only had the Jeep, so early one morning, the girls piled us all in Shirley's car and we set off for Virginia Beach, down through Richmond, with the two Moms in the front seat giggling and laughing about things that forty-year-old girls giggle and laugh about.

All of the windows were down, because there was no air conditioning in cars then, so I really couldn't hear what the women were saying, but a lot of it was interrupted with laughing. Both women smoked, so even with the windows down, the car was still smoky. When we arrived in Virginia Beach, everyone put on their bathing suits and splashed and sunned. I had been to the ocean at Assateague, but this was a "Beach" beach. This place was full of people dressed in "not much." A French engineer had introduced his "bikini" design to the public in 1946 when cloth was scarce after WWII. The general design had been around for over a thousand years, but he named his very skimpy design "bikini" for the Bikini Atoll, the island where atomic bombs were being tested by the US after WWII. The religious communities all over the world came out against it, and, of course by doing so, made it extremely popular. When a very fully developed young woman came by us wearing a tiny, skimpy version, I heard Mom mumble to Aunt Shirley,

"My dish rag is bigger than what that woman has on."

The Moms giggled. I stifled mine. By the time we got home late that night it had been a long day, but we all had enjoyed it, especially the Moms.

My older half-brother, Jerry, was eighteen when he drove to Virginia from Hamlin, WV in his 1941 Studebaker to spend part of the summer with us. That summer he took me to my first (but certainly not last) organized stock car race. On a couple of occasions Dad took his three boys to work and dropped us off in Downtown DC for the day. We walked up the Washington Monument the first time, but we decided we didn't need to do that again, so the next time we went there, we rode the elevator up, and walked and ran down.

Because he only took us a few times, during the week when we were at home, Jerry, six-year-old Jim, and I, eleven years old, worked around the farm during the day while Dad was working as the attorney for Washington National Airport, known today as Reagan National. Jan was at Oma Lena's house while Mom worked in a cellophane factory in Fredericksburg.

It was standard practice back then for government employees to receive gifts from lobbyists, until Sherman Adams, Eisenhower's chief of staff, was given a very expensive vicuna fur coat from some lobbyist. Adams was fired. Regulations were made to prevent government employees from receiving gifts from anyone. Or maybe the rules were there but no one obeyed them. I don't know.

So.... Before Sherman Adams got in trouble, Dad had received a big wicker picnic basket full of eight bottles of Haig and Haig pinch-bottle, fifteen-year-old scotch whiskey from one of the companies involved in transporting people from the airport after they landed. There were city cabs, and Hertz Rent-A-Car, and Airport Transit Company, like a cab company, but it only picked up or dropped off at the airport. Avis wanted to establish their rent-a-car company at the airport, but there was resistance. In 1951, Dad thought that one rent-a-car company at the airport was enough. I don't know where the scotch came from, but it was an impressive gift, and Dad loved it. One bottle of fifteen-year-old pinch today will run about sixty dollars.

Dad savored it. He took a drink or two on Saturday nights after a day riding that mower as I pulled it through the fields with the Jeep or building thousands of feet of beautiful oak board fencing along our lane through the fields. But that was all. I think one of those bottles might have lasted two months or more. That is until Jerry saw it.

So, while Mom was working in Fredericksburg, Jerry, Jim, and I were on our own that week. Jerry, Jim, and I were painting the oak fence along the lane in the hot Virginia sun. We came into the house to make our lunch at noon, and Jerry saw the bottle of scotch.

"Let's have a drink of scotch," he said.

"Yeah, but Dad will know!" I protested.

"We'll put water in to hide it. He'll never know."

"Ok."

And we did. Jerry poured some of the scotch into our two glasses of RC Cola, our official house soft drink in those days, and added water to hide our pilferage. Jim said he didn't want any.

It wasn't bad. Not like the beer I had tasted a couple of months earlier, when Mom let me have a taste of hers. I didn't like it, and I had said,

"Yuck."

"Remember that." Mom had said.

The next day Jerry and I did the same thing. And the next couple of days. The bottle looked just as it had at the beginning of the week.

Saturday night came.

Dad had his drink.

We sat down at the table for dinner. Dad was at the head of the table, Jerry on his right. I was on his left; Jim sat beside me. Mom at the other end, with Jan in her highchair next to Mom. Dad started the conversation.

"Someone's been drinking my scotch."

My blood ran cold.

He looked at the three of us. It was quieter than anything you can imagine. His cold blue eyes took in the table, pausing longer at Jerry and me. I probably would have been two inches taller my entire life if he hadn't stared at me so long.

"So, who was it?"

It was very quiet for an hour.... Maybe half a minute. It was a long, long, long time. I could hear a cricket chirping in the pantry. Finally I spoke in a very quiet voice.

"I had some."

"Alright, then you can have some more."

He got up and filled an eight ounce water glass with the

remainder of the bottle of scotch and put it in front of me.

"Drink this before you eat."

It was quieter than midnight on a frosty night. No one moved as I drank the scotch while everyone stared at me. I expected to be sick, but I wasn't. I didn't feel anything at all, except the misery of being caught in a scheme, and my brother, Jerry, who started it, was getting off free. Adding the water had tipped off Dad, and it was weak enough that it didn't bother me. I realize that Dad knew Jerry was the cause of the whole scene, but it was enough to make an example of me, and anyway, Jerry hadn't admitted that he had drunk any. In my mind, I took one for the team, but Jerry was eighteen, and the oldest. He owed me, Big Time.

I can't really call that a strike on Mom, but it certainly wasn't a hit. I guess it was an error on my part.

The third strike for Mom came later.... snakes. You can't have a farm in Virginia without snakes. My sister, Jan, tells about that adventure:

"Snakes were a worrisome concern on the farm. There were water moccasins in the pond, copperheads in the woods, and black snakes in the pantry. Soon after we moved in and got the phone, Mom went into the pantry and came face to face with a big black snake hanging from the rafters. She screamed and ran out, grabbing me on the way. As soon as she caught her breath, she returned to the house and called the O'Brien boys, (adult men, but they were known as "boys" in our house), who were neighbors about a mile away, and in a panicked voice asked them to come and kill the snake. They

arrived a while later with their .22 rifle and shot the snake while Mom and I waited in the yard. They found and killed five more snakes in the pantry that day."

The snakes put major questions in Mom's mind. She had seen snakes outside, but never in the ceiling in the house. The pantry was a dark place with an unfinished ceiling that connected to the ceiling in the kitchen and the living room. Did the O'Brien's get them all? Were there snakes somewhere that they couldn't see? Will the snakes fall through the ceiling in the kitchen that wasn't drywalled, but instead had battens of insulation hanging there, held up by a few lathes? Have snakes moved to other places in the house?

Mom really tried hard to make life on the farm work, but she was unprepared for things this life threw at her. One day, time got away from her and she realized she had forgotten to put the dried beans on the electric stove to cook, so she put them in the pressure cooker to cook them quicker for dinner and turned the stove on high heat. In about fifteen minutes, there was an enormous "BOOM," and beans flew all over the stove, on the walls, and into the uncovered insulation in the ceiling. Husks from cooking the dried beans apparently had clogged the steam hole in the lid, and the pressure had built up inside the pot, blowing the lid off of the pressure cooker. As the beans cooled they dropped down onto whatever was under them, countertops, floors, dishes, people, but for some reason some stayed up there and the next day, beans still fell from the ceiling. As kids, Jim and I laughed, but Mom didn't.

My eighth grade teacher, Mrs. Woolfolk, was a wonderful person. She must have been a baseball fan because she let us listen to the World Series in class. I had all the friends I could stand, (including Billy) and I was enjoying school. What, Mark? "**It's what you know for sure that just ain't so.**"

West Virginia Again

One night I dreamed that Mom told me I was going to go back to my grandparents in West Virginia to live. Less than a week later, she sat me down and told me that I was going back to West Virginia to spend the balance of my eighth grade there. The thought of this was a mixed bag for me. I loved my grandparents but I had left that life a long time ago in my mind. I had friends. I would have to make new friends again. Living in West Virginia was a totally different lifestyle to me now, and I wasn't sure if I would like it.

She and Dad were taking Jim and Jan back to DC to live in an apartment since the late fall and winter hardships on the farm were going to be more than she could handle. Dad typically left the house at 5:30 for his morning commute after Mother fixed him eggs and bacon, with his RC Cola, (he seldom drank coffee), and he never got home until after 7 at night when we would eat dinner. The old farmhouse would be cold this winter. It was a lot for her to handle by herself.

So, I filled one of Mom's suitcases with some clothes and went to DC with Dad where I got on a small passenger plane, probably a DC-3, and flew to Charleston, WV, landing at the Kanawha County Airport, now called Yeager Airport, honoring Chuck Yeager. I'll tell you about him in a minute. From the airport, I took a taxi to the Greyhound bus station in downtown Charleston, and as planned, got on the afternoon bus with the destination sign that said "Richmond." The bus went 40 miles upstream beside the Kanawha River through Gauley Bridge, where the Kanawha begins at the convergence of the New River and the Gauley River. From there the bus drove up through the mountains to Ansted. My parents had written to my grandparents to meet the bus that I was on, because my grandparents didn't have a phone. When I got to Ansted, Grandad was there in his almost-new 1952 International pickup truck to take me to Ramsey. After we got off of the Midland Trail (Rt. 60), he let me drive the Saturday Road.

Apparently Mother had done some negotiating. The one room schools were still open, but I was to attend Ansted Elementary, so I rode the high school bus that dropped me off and picked me up at the elementary School. The driver was Lyle Ramsey, the son of Anson, my sixth grade teacher at Cavendish. I was the only elementary student on the bus. If you're keeping track, I had just turned twelve, and this was school number seven.

Once again, I was "the new kid on the block," well, this time, "on the mountain." Since these kids had been together all their lives, a new kid from Virginia was not quickly accepted, and to them, I talked funny. Plus, some Mountaineer people don't accept new people very easily. On the other hand, my teachers knew my grandad, since they'd gone to teachers' meetings together for years. I can imagine some of the scuttlebutt that circulated around them about "Melvin's daughter's boy."

When I arrived, the classes were being held in an old wooden two-story school building behind the new school which hadn't been finished. Within a month or two, everyone moved into the new school. The basketball court for the old school was a flat spot on the hillside with a floor of bare soil, no grass, and a hoop without a net, attached to a telephone pole. As I write this, it's the last year for this school to be open, according to people who live there

I joined the 4-H Club and made a pair of bookends in the old store building at Grandad's for my project. I learned some things by doing that. Primarily, I learned that I was not a carpenter or furniture maker. I gave the bookends to my grandparents, who kept them with a few books in the living room where the ugly, but loved things stayed as long as they lived in the house.

I spend several Sundays at Aunt Sybil's, playing with my three cousins, and one of her neighbors' sons, Charlie McCoy. Charlie was a year and a half younger than me, and I guess he still is, but he grew up to be a top performing country music harmonica player playing for Johnny Cash, Ann Margaret, and a bunch of people. For years, he was the music director for the Hee Haw TV show. But I could beat him in croquet. Check him out on YouTube.

While we're talking about famous people, Jim and I had something in common with Chuck Yeager, the person the airport is named after. Chuck is one of West Virginia's most famous people because he was a WWII fighter pilot Ace, and the first person to officially fly faster than sound. He was one of the instructors for the astronauts. But the thing he, Jim, and I have in common is that Dad whipped all three of us. Dad taught Chuck in elementary school. Chuck was shooting spitballs, and Dad saw him and whipped him. As an officer in the Pentagon told Dad on our tour, Dad is probably one of the only people in the world who ever whipped Chuck Yeager.

In 1952, after the school year ended, I went to 4-H camp for a week in West Virginia. In the camp activity center, the kids who could dance, danced while a jukebox played the hit of the summer, Kay Starr singing ***Wheel of Fortune***. At night we sat around a big campfire with circular stands for the kids to sit on, as we sang songs, and the counselors told us spooky stories. I was old enough not to get caught up in them, but they were good. Someone told me that people from West Virginia are good storytellers, but who am I to judge? I met a girl named Imogene, a tall and slender girl that I wanted to know better. We hung out together when possible, and managed a few hugs and kisses after the campfire stories. Her kisses gave me the strongest funny feelings inside me that I had ever had. When I got back to the farm, I realized we had separated and gone home on Friday without getting addresses, or having any way to stay in touch.

Saturday morning Grandad took me to Ansted to catch the 7:30 morning Greyhound Bus headed to Richmond that would stop in Lexington, Va, where I would change over to the Trailways Bus Lines to go to Orange, since the family had moved back to the farm. That trip would take at least 14 hours, and it would be dark when I got to Orange. The bus stop in Ansted was at the new town drugstore, owned by the parents of one of my eighth grade classmates, Ben Linkenhoker. Ben was the only one running the store that morning, and no customers came in while I was there. As Ben and I sat at the soda fountain and talked for fifteen or twenty minutes, he would stick a small piece of wire in the slot of the selection box to activate the jukebox. When he played the same song, ***C'est si bon,*** over and over again, I became an Eartha Kitt fan.

Back in Virginia

When I arrived in Orange that night the family was there to pick me up. I discovered Mom and Dad were peeved, because they thought I was coming home the week before. Apparently, my grandparents hadn't written to tell my parents I was in camp, or perhaps the letter didn't arrive in time, so every night for a week, everyone had driven forty miles to and from the bus stop in Orange to pick me up.

The next morning at the farm, I discovered Dad had contracted with an earth-moving contractor in Orange, to build an acre-and-a-half pond down the hill from the house and it was filling up with water from the stream that ran through the bottom of the field. Dad had installed four long poles and several shorter ones before the water was allowed to accumulate. He built a thirteen-foot-high diving board at the end of a twenty-foot pier. The pond was thirteen feet deep at the end of the pier, so it was twenty-six feet to the bottom of the pond from the top. Mom quickly taught Jim and me how to dog-paddle, and we improved our swimming over the summer. It was a major challenge for Jim and me to dive off the top and go all the way to the cold bottom and come back up to fresh air. Dad brought a rowboat from Sears along with a two-wheeled trailer to be pulled by the tractor, and we assembled both.

The cart's wheels always wobbled when we pulled it with the tractor.

That summer, Dad bought a new Ford 8N tractor, along with a Bush-Hog mower, and a disc harrow and we moved on. No more Jeep pulling a mower with a rider. If the tractor could push down the brush or little trees, the

Bush-Hog would grind it up.

I loved mowing with the Bush-Hog. You could sit on the tractor and because you were driving slowly, think about anything in the world. There was no gas pedal. The driver moved a lever to set the amount of gas that was constantly supplied to the engine. The driver chose the gear and the amount of gas needed for the strength and speed the tractor needed to do the job. Then all the driver did was to steer in a field where steering was not usually that critical. It was very nice. But not always.....

There were these little black and yellow fuzzy bees, called bumblebees that built nests in the ground. As I drove up a hill, in low gear at a very slow speed to give me the torque I wanted, I mowed over a nest of them. Several thousand came out. Well, I didn't count them, but there were a lot and they were attacking me. I felt like it lasted a long time, but it was probably a half minute before I could drive out of them. I don't remember how many stings I had, but I know I had eight stings just on my face, plus a lot on my arms and legs. They hurt terribly. The next morning, I went to school with a face swollen way beyond its normal size.

The tractor is made to work in the fields, but sometimes it balks if the ground is too soggy. I got into trouble mowing near a creek where the ground was so soggy the tractor buried the large rear wheels in it and spun the tires. I walked to the house and got Dad, (fortunately, it was on a weekend). He brought the Jeep down with a log chain, and hooked it to the tractor with the Jeep on dry ground. The Jeep spun all four tires, as the tractor spun its two tires, but the tractor didn't move. Dad walked back to the house and got Mom and the car and drove it down through the field above the Jeep. We hooked another chain from the Jeep to the car, and Mom drove the car, Dad drove the Jeep, I drove the tractor, all the wheels went round, and round, and the tractor came out. Ok, I spun a yarn ending in a sing-song kindergarten song, but it's what happened.

If you own a farm tractor, you don't want to have to drive it to a gas station eight miles away every time it needs gasoline, so what do you do? You make a deal with a gasoline distributor to sell or loan you a tank and pump so they can sell you a couple hundred gallons of gasoline at a time. So, that's what Dad did. The distributor brought the bright red 200 gallon tank and placed it on the top of the ground next to the road to the barn. The driver installed a hand-cranked pump to the top of the tank, and filled it with Ethyl, the nickname for gasoline that contained lead. Lead was in gasoline in the US from the '20's until around the mid '80's, poisoning everyone who smelled gasoline or inhaled the fumes. The gas was supposed to be for the tractor, so it was cheaper than gas at the service station, since there were no state or federal road taxes on it, plus you bought it in bulk, not five dollars at a time. It was my job every night to go out and take the '52 Nash to the gas tank, fill it with fuel, check the oil, and wipe the windshield after Dad got home from his 175-mile-round trip to and from work. The car always smelled of cigar smoke. This was one of my favorite jobs.

As I said earlier, Mom showed me how to iron Dad's shirts, after they were washed in the washing machine, and hung outside to dry on a clothesline, but she usually ironed Dad's shirts, That is, until there was Lucille.

When Mom started working in a cellophane factory in Fredericksburg, she hired Lucille to clean the house, cook, do the laundry and watch Jan when school opened.

Lucille was actually a next-door neighbor, through the forest, but with the roads she probably drove her 1950 Studebaker four miles to our house.

Lucille was a wonderful person in the eyes of Jim and me. She had six or seven of her own kids and wasn't easily shaken, so she took a bunch of burdens from Mom, Jim, and me. She often stood over the stove, stirring a pot of beans or boiling chicken, smoking a Camel cigarette with an ash that seemed to be two inches long.

Jim and I thought the ash would surely fall into the pot, but to our knowledge never did.

It seemed to me that the whole world smoked except Jim and me. Over 40% of the population used tobacco. In high school there was a smoking area outside the school for kids. Teachers had the teacher's lounge that dumped smoke into the hall when the door was opened. You could smoke in the rear of an airplane, in an office, in a restaurant, or in a hospital room.Tobacco companies hired doctors to sell their cigarettes. Basically, you could smoke almost anywhere, except where there was a chance of a fire or an explosion. Even families that did not have any smokers had ashtrays. Dad smoked a pipe or El Producto cigars. Mom was smoking Pall Malls now, instead of Herbert Tareytons. Occasionally I smoked a few of Mom's longer cigarette stubs that I would find in the ashtrays. I once persuaded Jim to take a puff from one, when we were out under the big pear tree, behind the old cabin which was now a garden shed. Jim says that one puff made him realize that he didn't want to smoke, so he never did. Naturally, now I can take some credit for keeping Jim tobacco-free for life. On the other hand, it put me on the road to a habit that led me to smoke for fifty years.

In September,1952, I went to the ninth grade at a different school, Orange County High School, a new school that was completed while I was in West Virginia. It was in the town of Orange but this time there were the students and Mrs. Woolfolk from my old class in Unionville, so it wasn't quite a totally new group.

As a brand new school, in 1952, we students, from all over the county, got to name all of the sports teams (The Hornets), the yearbook (Golden Horseshoe), and school colors (orange and blue). Thousands of students have followed these colors and names since we named them that fall, over 70 years ago.

Our school bus drivers were mostly students who were at least 18 years old. The buses had governors on them to keep the speeds under 55, maybe 60 if it was going downhill.

I want to tell you about Robert

Probably my best friend at Orange High was Robert Shipley. Robert had fiery red hair. Most of his world called him "Red," and he adopted the nickname. Some say it was Football Coach Sizemore, who first gave him his nickname. That's probably right, but I never called him "Red." More about Coach Sizemore in a minute.

All through high school Robert and I were close friends. The Shipley family lived about two miles from our farm, in a huge old farmhouse even bigger than ours. Every school day, Robert got on the almost-empty school bus before me and took one of the back seats. BTW, the School Board had retired our old wooden bus, and switched to steel. Next, up the gravel road David stopped to pick up Betty Jane (fake name), Robert's very attractive blond-haired girlfriend through most of our high school years. She sat next to the window beside Robert. The next stop was about a mile up the road where Jim and I got on. Jim sat near the front. I went to the back and sat across the aisle from Robert. David turned left to head toward Orange. After he picked up a bus full of children, he dropped Jim and the elementary children off at Unionville Elementary and drove us to Orange.

Generally we talked about the Orange County High football team, which Robert played on for a year or two, discussed country music, or told our latest jokes. No one was immune from our sarcasm. No one had cell phones in the fifties, or even a portable radio. These things weren't around until after the invention of the transistor in the sixties. We just joked, laughed and talked. Robert had an excellent vocabulary, and he loved to show it off with his deep voice. His favorite word was "indubitably," which he used every time he could. It means "undoubtedly." He was born in Tennessee and his Tennessee roots showed in his speech, having a little more mountain than southern accent, although the South was in there too. He was smart but not a gifted student, even though he had good language skills.

Robert lived with his mother, Oma Lena, her husband, A.L., their adult daughter, Jewell, and her daughter, Priscilla, who was a year younger than Jim, and an adult brother, Jack. Our mothers were close friends, which meant that often Mother would pile us in the Jeep and go to Oma Lena's for a visit, using the excuse she wanted to borrow a cup of sugar, or something, but likely she was bored and tired. When we went to the Shipleys, Jim and Jan would play with Priscilla, and Robert and I would hurry up the stairs to his room, open a window, light up cigarettes, listen to country music, and plan our future as radio announcers. We would critique the announcers, singers, DJ's and boast about our own prowess.

Our own prowess hadn't even been developed yet. Heck, we didn't even know what prowess was.

Country music was hard core then. No Taylor Swift, No Clay Walker. Not even Brooks and Dunn. Just people like Kitty Wells, Bill Monroe, Hank Snow, and a young girl just starting her career, Patsy Cline. It was a big deal in country music when in 1952, Kitty Wells came out with the song, **"God Didn't Make Honky-Tonk Angels."** She was answering Hank Thompson's song, **"The Wild Side of Life,"** where he said he didn't know God made honky-Tonk Angels. Kitty's hit was the first time a woman had ever reached the number one spot on Billboard's country charts.

Rock and Roll had started but it hadn't matured yet, so pop music was still in vogue. We both liked pop as well as country, but we worshiped bluegrass and country music in Robert's room.

One week, WJMA, the local radio station in Orange, VA, offered an hour slot at night where high school students could be DJ's playing pop music for a week. Robert and I each took a week playing records and reading the news and weather.For five straight nights Dad had to take me and wait in Orange until my time was up, and take me home. He did, and never complained, so "Thank you, Dad" for that. I remember the big song during my week was "Mr. Sandman," sung in harmony by the Chordettes, four older women from Wisconsin. I played it every night the week I was on the air.

One year it was student's day at the station, and four or five students were DJ's all day. We couldn't do the beer commercials, but on that day, we students did all the other announcing. Robert had a morning session. I had an evening slot, so I was reading the 6 PM news. The station's announcers operated on the rip-and-read system, which meant the announcer would rip the latest news off of the teletype machine, and read it on the air right away, so that's what I did. I ripped the sports news off the machine and started reading on the air. I read a story about baseball player Ted Williams and his estranged wife. I had never seen the word "estranged" before, and I read it as his "estrangled wife." The engineer in the booth opposite me began laughing. I saw him laughing through the glass windows, and I started laughing on the air in a serious part of the news. I finished the sports and did the rest of my broadcast. It was not the professional image I wanted.

Robert made it big time.

A couple of years later, I went to college in Richmond during the days and wound up working evenings and nights as a cameraman at WRVA-TV. I was never an announcer. For reasons I will tell you about later, I didn't see Robert for three years after my senior year. When I next saw him in Fredericksburg, he was morning DJ, and afternoon salesman, at the station in Warrenton. A few years later, I visited Robert when he was the morning DJ and program manager at WPIK in Alexandria, VA, the top country station in the DC area, but our early bonds had dissolved, and I was out of the broadcasting industry, so we went our separate ways, and I never saw him again.

Robert became very popular in Northern Virginia, and DC, and was considered a legend in the business. He received national awards as a DJ, and was regarded as one of the very best in the business. Once he appeared on "Hee Haw," alongside the musical director of the show, Charlie McCoy, who as I said, lived near my aunt. Robert passed away about ten years ago. I knew he had made it big, but I didn't know how big until I read his obituary years later. Google Robert (Red) Shipley for more on him.

Mr.Taylor taught me and the agriculture students, and was the sponsor of the FFA, (Future Farmers of America). I also belonged to the 4-H Club. I went to one club's summer camp one year, and the other club's the next year at their campgrounds. One year I went to a week-long 4H Club state-wide conference held at VPI in Blacksburg, VA. Mom had attended one of these when she was young, in West Virginia, so I felt I was carrying on a family tradition. There, I and two other boys, my school bus driver, David, and Wayne, represented our 4H district, made up of four or five counties, as the district poultry-judging team. We had won the District contest, because we were really good, but David came down with the mumps at the conference, and while Wayne and I competed by judging live poultry and candling eggs to check for freshness, there were only two of us competing against teams of three. Because our scores weren't high enough to place, we finished last, but I can still tell you if a hen is or isn't laying eggs.

I won the county 4-H poultry-raising contest that year. I was the only person to keep my chickens in individual cages. It was a new way to increase egg production, and foxes and dogs couldn't bother the chickens. Years later the trend has changed back to the same way everyone raised them for thousands of years, but now they call them free-range chickens and everyone says that is the way to go. One of my hens won an honorable mention at the Virginia State Fair, known then as the Atlantic Rural Exposition, in Richmond.

At the conference I entered a public speaking competition, but I didn't win. I was in a debate contest but I lost the debate. We learn when we lose. Right?

I entered the county 4-H tractor driving contest one year. Part of the test required the driver to back a ten-foot manure spreader down a very narrow path inches wider than the spreader, without touching the guide lines until the tractor and spreader would both be in the barn. I won the country award but to win the district contest, one had to be fourteen. Remember, I had been driving a tractor for over five years, so it was not my first rodeo. (tractor rodeo, sorta.) Since I won the county contest, the 4-H coordinator said I should go to the district contest for practice. I participated in the district contest but I was disqualified for my age. I wouldn't have won, anyway, but it was good practice. We learn when we lose. Oh, I just said that! Heck, it seemed that I was losing a lot but I was in the contests. One year my project was bees. It taught me about bees, but it didn't make me a beekeeper. It made me realize that the world needs bees to pollinate fruits and vegetable plants for our food supplies. I don't even kill bumblebees, after what they did to me.

The summer I was fourteen, I went to a 4-H camp at Holiday Lake, near Appomattox. On the way, near Lexington, we got out of the school bus to walk down to see the Natural Bridge. During that week, we rode the bus to Appomattox to see where Lee surrendered to Grant. We swam in Holiday Lake. The boys stayed in cabins on a rise on one side of a large, flat playing area that went down to the lake, and over a hundred yards away, the girls had cabins on the other side, also on a small hill. It was that camp that I learned to play Box Hockey. Box Hockey is played in a wooden box made from boards or plywood, sitting on the ground, about three feet wide, and six feet long with holes in both ends and two holes on each side in a center board, that divides the box into two sides. The holes allow you to get the rock into the opponent's territory. Place a rock on the center board and using an ax handle, hold the hockey stick against your opponent to a count of three, and try to put the rock through the opponent's outer board's hole. You score a point when you knock the rock out of your opponent's box onto the ground.

A girl in my class, Jane (Fake Name), a tall lanky girl, was there with me. I never got to see her much at camp, since it seems we did boy things and girls did girl things, but on the bus ride home we became closer but we didn't glue tightly together, and she lived in town, and I lived halfway to hell and back, so after the trip home, the glue melted and we went our separate ways when school started.

Dad bought about ten head of Black Angus cattle, after we fixed up the fences around the fields where they could roam. I was accustomed to the gentleness and friendliness of white-faced Herefords in West Virginia. The Black Angus herd Dad bought wasn't gentle or friendly. They weren't particularly aggressive, but they had wandering in their DNA. It was not unusual to have to go find them and drive them back to our fields. I remember once they found a weak place in the fence and wandered out of the farm along the electric power lines. I went to find them and drive them home. I missed the school bus, so I did not learn those things that were taught that day in Orange. Missing that day is why I don't

know all the things I should know today..... Ok, maybe not.
One class that I enjoyed was the once-a-month Phys Ed class where the boys and girls met together in the gym to learn all types of dancing, including slow dancing, waltz, jitterbug, square dancing, the Virginia Reel, and the Grand March. Even though these dances don't seem to be in use now, the Virginia Reel was seen in movies in the '50's based in the South, and the Grand March was in movies about debutantes coming into society, so we were taught how to do them. In the slow dances It was exciting to be able to hold the girl that sat next to you in history. I don't know if the girls thought it was exciting, but I suspect some of them did, especially dancing with the boys who were the sports stars of the schools. .

I had fun in school, even though I had to take the bus home, and not get involved in after-school things, except very special events, because Mom or Dad would have to come get me, and I had work to do on the farm. I took band class and continued to play the trombone, but the school didn't have a marching band. During our senior year, in the fall, Robert practiced football after school, so I rode home without him. One time I sat down by an attractive junior girl and we began a conversation. I don't remember what it was about, but we both clicked, and from then on I sat with her. And we began to know each other. Her name was Julie, and she lived on a farm somewhere east of school, like me, but she got on another bus in 'Unionville, and so I don't really know exactly where she lived. We enjoyed each other but never dated.
Someone asked me,
"Have you ever played hooky?"

Once. (All names here are fake, because I don't remember who went with me.) One of my buddies, George, had a car so he offered to drive Bill, Randy, and me a few miles down the road toward Culpeper to show us the house thathadburnedthepreviousnight,Afterhomeroom.... (Do they even have "homerooms,"anymore?) We gathered in our homeroom, a classroom where we met every morning for ten minutes where attendance was taken, students said the pledge of allegiance, prayed and heard daily announcements, then we were dismissed and we individually went to our classes.) Anyway, after homeroom, we got into George's old Plymouth, and as soon as we left the school parking lot, Randy said,
"Man, we need some cigars," so George stopped at a general store and we went in to buy cigars. Bill said,
"I'm going to get a Marsh Wheeling. They're not big around and they're real sweet."

I had puffed on one of Dad's big El Producto cigar butts that I swiped from the ash tray, and I knew I didn't want an El Producto. The Marsh Wheelings were slender, and "sweet" sounded just right, plus they were cheap, so Bill and I each bought one. I don't remember what Randy and George bought. We lit up, piled back in the car and headed on. By the time we got to the burned house, I was burned out. The cigar was sweet, but in a sickeningly sweet way to me. The inside of the car stunk. My body rebelled. I wasn't even halfway through smoking it, but I threw it away when we stopped. Bill stayed with his smoke. The smoke filled the car. I didn't get sick, I just had a sick feeling all the way back to school. We arrived back in time for lunch. After lunch we went to our classes. Playing hooky wasn't that much fun. During my life, I smoked a lot of cigars. Marsh Wheeling wasn't one of them.

Screwing Up

When Mom started work Dad bought a new turquoise 1955 Plymouth Savoy,so Mom carpooled to Fredericksburg in the '52 Nash. I was allowed to drive the Jeep out the mile-long farm lane and park it near the public gravel road to catch the school bus. That is, until I screwed up.

We had that board fence two-tenths of a mile long between our front field and the dirt road from the front yard to where the woods began. It was a beautiful white fence with four horizontal oak boards nailed to four by six inch oak posts every eight feet. With the contrast between the white fence and the green pasture, it was beginning to look like a Gentleman Farmers pasture, but the Black Angus cows had gone, one to our rented freezer locker in Orange, the others to someone else's farm. Near the house was an eight-foot opening that gave us access to go into the field and down to the one acre pond.

One morning the Jeep wouldn't start. I figured with the tractor I could push the Jeep and by keeping it in gear, with the key turned off, it wouldn't start, so I could push it through the opening in the fence to where the slope would let me push the Jeep by hand toward the pond, get in it, turn the key on, pop the clutch, and start it. I got the tractor and slowly pushed the Jeep to the edge of the slope. But the Jeep kept moving slowly downhill toward the pond after I stopped pushing it.. I was on the tractor watching the Jeep going to the pond, and I panicked. I reached to turn the tractor's key off, but my fingers couldn't find the ignition key which is located under part of the hood on the 8N tractor. I couldn't lose the Jeep in the pond. I jumped off the tractor, ran, got in the Jeep, and stopped it.

I could hear the tractor running. I looked back and saw the tractor going in a big circle. It had a fence post jammed against the steering wheel and had taken down sixteen more feet of that beautiful white board fence. I took the post from the tractor, turned it off, and started the Jeep by coasting before popping the clutch. After I put the tractor away, I drove Jim and me to the school bus. The missing footage of the fence was obvious.

All that day, I dreaded the arrival of Dad that night. When he got home, I received a world-class chewing out by Dad,The Attorney. I was not allowed to drive the Jeep to the school bus for a month as punishment. As parents, Mom and Dad did an excellent job of punishing us. Of course, at the time, I didn't believe that, but basically, we were allowed to do what we wanted to do, but if we broke a rule, or did something totally foolish, there was usually swift corporal punishment, with a belt, or at least once, a stick of stove wood. Once Dad took me to the barn and literally beat me on my butt with an 18 inch-long stick of stove wood, about 2 inches in diameter. I don't remember what the punishment was for, but I remember I was sore for a day or so. Dad's booming courthouse voice could put fear in me, and of course, anticipation of punishment is always part of the punishment. In this case though, it meant no driving the jeep to the bus for a month. On those two-mile-a-day-walking trips, Jim and I developed our non-musical voices by singing hit parade songs, and some with silly things, such as, " Be kind to your web-footed friends, because a duck may be somebody's mother," a song that is sung to the tune from the ***Stars and Stripes Forever,*** written by the "March King, John Phillip Sousa.

Our English teacher was the football coach, Coach Sizemore. That's right, our English teacher. He was a friendly, fun guy. (Funguy? Fungi? Isn't that the plural of fungus?) We learned about....football. Yes, we did learn about Shakespeare and Dickens, but more than that, we learned about last Friday night's game, the game to come next Friday, and the games other teams had played. When a boy would miss a question in an impromptu personal one-question oral exam about anything in the world, he would be sent to the hall to do ten pushups. If he was on the football team, it was twenty push ups. If he was thin and frail, he only got five pushups. Girls didn't get any pushups. They got to laugh at the boys.

One cold morning after Mom left for work, Jim and I heard on the radio that county schools were closed because of snow. There would be no Lucille coming that day, because there was no school, so I was P.I.C, (person in charge). Not a good situation. Within an hour or so, after Mom left, Jim and I were goofing off, and I wound up chasing him down the stairs. At the bottom, he slipped and his head fell back against the wall, splitting it open on the corner of a door frame. It was bleeding profusely. I had a little first aid knowledge, as everyone does when they live on a farm, so I stopped the bleeding and put a bandage on it. Meanwhile it continued snowing in inches.

When Mom got home that night, the snow was so deep,

she left her car at the neighbors, and he brought her down our road on his tractor. She was not happy about Jim. She thought he needed stitches. Maybe he had a concussion. She called the neighbor who had brought her in, to come back and get her and Jim so she could take him to the doctor in Orange. The neighbor came and I watched Mom and Jim leave in the snow storm, perched on the fender of the cold tractor. I stayed with Jan, and in a couple of hours, she returned on the fender with Jim, who had a fresh bandage and a piece of what looked like the top of a woman's hosiery to hold the split skin together. She told me the doctor said it was too late to put stitches in the wound, and that he would have a scar, with no hair to cover it, which he did for years. Apparently there was no concussion. She and I were relieved. Her, from a couple of hours not knowing, me, from all day not knowing.

About an hour after she and Jim had returned, Dad called to tell her he was in a hotel in New York City, and to not worry about him. I didn't hear the conversation, but when she hung up, she exploded. "Ha! He told me not to worry about him!" as she used some of her sailors' language.

That episode was a major strike.

Family Reunions

One summer we hosted the annual Roberts' Family reunion. Dad was one of thirteen children, and with everyone married and having children of all ages, the annual reunion was a big event in Ohio where most of the members lived. Only about twenty people made the trip to our farm from Ohio and West Virginia, but it was enough for Mom, with everyone milling around in and out of the house. There was only one bathroom, and I don't remember any Porta-Potties being brought in, but there might have been one. Most people arrived Friday evening, the rest arrived Saturday morning. A few slept at our house. The rest went to motels around Orange.

There were green alligators and long-necked geese,,, No, wait, wrong thought. There were young cousins, older aunts and uncles and....Uncle Ralph. Uncle Ralph was married legally, but not practically. I always wondered how Uncle Ralph had picked that woman to be his wife. They never had children. But this year, Uncle Ralph, who was about sixty-five, brought a thirty-something lady who dressed very provocatively, with all the meanings of the word. Look it up, if you don't know them. When she played badminton in the side yard dressed in short shorts, and a top with a lot of skin showing, I was surprised at how many of the men were interested in badminton. The women had trouble with her being there. The men, not so much. I didn't have any problem with her at all.

Dad was not particularly religious, but he had installed a loudspeaker high on the corner of the house and hooked up a phonograph inside so that he could play old gospel records to the relatives outside. It was high tech in the '50's. My favorite song he played was ***I'll Fly Away*** by the Chuck Wagon Gang. I still like it.

Saturday morning Dad gathered the men together and took them to the far side of the pond to help him clear some brush near the pond. I'm fairly certain he never told the guys about the extra duty ahead of time, but I think the men enjoyed the camaraderie of being together working on a common chore. There was a discussion centered on politics, but not a lot of clearing got done. I remember the discussion about smoking cigarettes or a pipe, which Dad smoked because, as Dad told them,

"I can waste more time while I am fixing and lighting my pipe than you cigarette smokers can, so my pipe is a better choice for me."

The guys booed him when he said that.

That day, my young cousin, four-year-old Pam, who had just been warned by her mother to not get her hair wet, when she wanted to come to the pond where the boys were swimming after she was dressed. She ran to the edge of the pond and yelled to us,

"Boys, don't get your hair wet." We all laughed.

The competition between brothers was on display at the reunion. Dad was a big man, at 6-2, 265 pounds. He had been a star football player in college, but smaller, slender Uncle Ravenel, was now a pro golf coach at a college in Ohio. When he tried to teach Dad how to hit a tee ball, Uncle Ravenel, who weighed about 180 pounds, made it look so simple and easy. He would tee up and effortlessly hit it 250 yards or so into the field. With everyone watching, Dad couldn't make it happen and soon balked at trying. I later learned it's hard to hit a golf ball very far until you learn how. I think Uncle Ravenel was just trying to pay Dad back for some unresolved hazing earlier in their lives, by embarrassing his older brother in front of the family.

Naturally, it rained the day of the big picnic, and we had to move to the Mine Run Community Center about seven miles away to eat inside. All of the utensils and food had to be put in different cars and driven to a place that some drivers didn't know how to get there. It took a while, and a few things never got there, but it happened. The whole reunion was a burden for Mom to handle. How many strikes does a woman get, anyway?

If her life were a baseball game, the stadium would be empty, and the lights out by now.

The Good Life

The following year, 1954, I was fifteen, and I had my learner's permit to drive with a licensed driver beside me. The family reunion was in Cadiz, Ohio, at Uncle Ravenal's. Dad, Jim, and I went, but Mom and Jan stayed home, no doubt to have some time alone, and we drove up RT 522 to Breezewood to get on the Pennsylvania Turnpike, where Dad stopped. When we started again he told me to drive. I was thrilled. The Turnpike hadn't been completed many years before, and it seemed to me to be a marvelous road. I gave the steering wheel back to Dad near Irwin, and he drove on into Pittsburgh. Even in the middle of the afternoon, the smoke and smog was so thick from the steel mills downtown that everyone had their lights on in the traffic. The smog was a memory that I never forgot, and the memory continues to remind me that we must work to keep our air and water clean. Driving on the PA Turnpike for the first time was the beginning of a lifetime of driving it, as I had customers all over the state a few years later, when I was living in Harrisburg. Later I used it frequently from living in Suburban Philadelphia, Ohio and Chicagoland. I became life-long friends with Breezewood since my daughter was living in Hagerstown.

That was the summer I went to the FFA (Future Farmers of America), and the FHA, (Future Homemakers of America) camp, somewhere around Surry, Va. It was like the usual summer camp until we went to Jamestown and Williamsburg. We got on the bus and drove to the James River. Our driver drove the bus onto a small ferry boat as we stayed on the bus. I think the bus was the only vehicle on the ferry. We rode across the James River to Jamestown, and toured Jamestown. Then, we went on to Williamsburg, to see the town as it must have looked in the 1760's. On the trip back to camp, I sat by Betsy, (not her real name), like me, a senior, who was going to her last FHA camp. Betsy was a slender, short girl, but like everyone in my class had developed into an attractive young adult. Well, maybe I hadn't developed that much. I never felt that I was very attractive, even after Marleen (fake name) showed some interest in me. I'll tell you about Marleen in a minute. I knew Betsy from school, as I did all the kids on the bus, but she had been dating a boy for a couple of years, so I had considered her as unapproachable. As we talked while returning to camp after crossing the James River on the bus again, her smiling face and sparkling brown eyes tormented me. When we got back to camp, we drifted off by ourselves. We held hands and walked closely together. After the first kiss there were several more, each sloppier than before. The following day, we went home on the bus together. That school year she was still dating her boyfriend. We spoke when we passed each other in the halls, but we never spent any time together.

I first saw Marleen (fake name) as she came into Mr. Willis's ninth grade Science class. We were all gangly in the ninth grade, except Maureen. She was a townie girl with a sense of regalness about her that said "I am the Queen." She was heavier than most of the other girls, but she carried herself in a way that was regal. I had occasionally danced with her during the Phys Ed classes, but I felt I was certainly not worthy of approaching the Queen, so we didn't really know each other until the beginning of my senior year when Dad dropped me off at a dance at the Grange Hall in Unionville. It was not a school dance, but one put on by the Grange, a national group made up mostly of farmers. For reasons unknown, Marleen was there.

I knew Marleen was intelligent, and now she had "filled out." I, too, had "filled out." "Filled out" means a lot of things, but relative to the two of us, it means she had gotten a little taller and had become a well-proportioned woman. She had adopted some of the appearances and attitudes– I said, some–not all, of America's female superstar in the fifties, Marilyn Monroe, including the blond hair, the red lipstick, and the way she walked. For me, I had gotten a little taller, standing at six feet, and weighing 165. I remember, because I had looked at playing football and coming home with Robert, but I couldn't catch or throw a football with any regularity, like Robert could, and I wasn't heavy enough to play a lineman,but I had developed a tanned body and a couple of muscles from working on the farm. Someone said that I reminded them of Tab Hunter, an actor and singer who was big stuff in those days. It must have been my looks, because I couldn't sing. As I told you, I had trouble just talking on the radio.

Since there were not many people there that we knew, she and I held each other and became closer as we danced the night away, in the brightly lit Granger Hall while Dean Martin sang his songs on his L-P record. Yeah, I know, "brightly lit," isn't exactly romantic, but I guess the Grangers didn't want to encourage any funny stuff. Even so, all that night I had that little fluttery thing going off in my insides..

A week or two later, after Ms. Kane's algebra class, my friend, Edmond, asked me "Did Betty invite you to her party?" (Fake name)

"No. When is it?"

"A week from Friday,"

"Doggone it," I said. " Dad just took me to the Granger dance. He's not going to want to take me to Gordonsville to a party."

"Why don't you spend the night with me? I'll drive us to the party, and your folks can pick you up at my house the next morning?"

"Yeah, that's a great idea!"

So, that's how I got to go to Betty's party. Later that day, Betty invited me. There were four boys and four girls at the party, held in Betty's basement.

Betty greeted us dressed in a pleated skirt and saddle shoes with her hair in a pony tail. She gave Ed and me hugs, Ed's hug, longer than mine, and took us into the basement. There were only eight people at the party. Ed and I represented half of the boys. Betty's mom and dad were ensconced upstairs in the living room. I was happily surprised to see Marleen was one of the girls. It didn't take long for the party to dissolve into a long game of “Spin the Bottle.” I had never played it. I didn’t even know what it was about. Betty spun the bottle. As she spun it I didn’t know what happened if someone won the spin, but at the time it looked like the spin was rigged. Marleen won. Betty took her through the door to the unfinished part of the basement where it was dark, and came back.

“Marleen would like to see Richard.” She announced louder than I thought she needed to. “Get up, Richard. Go see what she wants.”

I got up and went back through the door. When I went in, Marleen closed the door and grabbed me. I wasn’t totally stupid, so I quickly hugged her and we kissed for what seemed to be half an hour, but it still wasn’t enough. We came back to the group and sat down with my heart pounding. That fluttery thing was really going off. Betty spun and she won and called for Edmond. In a few spins Marleen won again. And I was called again. When I won, I called for Marleen. As I said, I’m not totally stupid. Because there were only four girls with four boys and the party lasted three hours, everyone won a lot. I never played Spin the Bottle again in my life, but I learned that girls can arrange the best parties you could ever want. The fluttery thing lasted for days.

At the end of my sophomore year, at age fourteen, I wanted to serve as Treasurer of the Student Government Association during my junior year. I asked a sparkly senior cheerleader, Sarah, if she would be my campaign manager. She accepted and worked like a beaver, putting my name on posters all over the school. It was a flattering couple of weeks seeing these posters. Because she sparkled, she got me elected.

The following year I ran for President of the Student Body. I had another sparkly cheerleader as my campaign manager. She sparkled too, but I was defeated by our school's star football player. Instead, my classmates elected me President of the Senior Class. I was fifteen years old when I was elected. That October I turned sixteen. I'm pretty sure that I was the youngest Senior Class President that had been elected, since there had only been three Senior Class Presidents at Orange County High before me. Maybe I still hold that title today. Who knows? I was a happy guy. I was going to have a wonderful year. What, Mark?

It's what you know for sure that just ain't so."

FARMALL

Ford

Saturday Rd 3
Sunday Rd 4
Leander Rd 3/2

Part Four

Fredericksburg

I was booking forward to a good Christmas when I came home on December 15th for Christmas holidays my senior year. Mother told me that Jim and I would not be going back to school in Orange County after the holidays. I could not go back to where I was Senior Class President. I couldn't get my books, clean out my locker, or even say goodbye to Marleen or any of my friends. Dad had moved to DC, and we were moving to Fredericksburg. I was really angry, and upset.

"Can I live with Robert until I graduate?"

"No!! You're coming with me."

" But Mom!! Oma Lena will let me!"

"NO, I said.!! You're coming with me."

"Mom! I've got to stay. I'm the Class President!"

I don't care if you're the President of the United States, You're coming with me. Now shut up before I slap you.."

I did, but I laid awake in bed that night still mad and frustrated, thinking about everything.

Today everyone has a cell phone, but in those days guys like me, living in the country, seldom called anyone. I never had anyone's phone number, so It was disheartening, and a rough Christmas for me. I was respected by my peers in high school. I would start over as the new student in a school where I didn't know anyone. I was tired of plowing new ground in my field of dreams.

On January 3, 1956, I was still pissed. Mother was entering me as a graduating senior in James Monroe High School in Fredericksburg, the archenemy of Orange High in sports and scholastic events. It was my ninth different school that I had attended. I was sixteen, but I had only lived with my parents for the past six years, and one of those had been interrupted for eight months. I felt, as every teenager feels, parents aren't always right. Mother and Dad had separated around Christmas. I understand now that Mother was burned out. The farm was too much for Mom and apparently Dad had been misbehaving with a neighbor, but I knew nothing about any of that. I was not mature enough to figure out how devastated she was from all the hardships she had endured on the farm, and now she had a deteriorating relationship with Dad.

Mother had rented an inexpensive two bedroom "shotgun apartment." A "shotgun apartment" means if you shoot a shotgun into the house at the front door, the shot will go out the back door without hitting anything. It was a popular small, inexpensive floor plan in the South. Mom said it best,

"You can't even cuss a cat in here without getting hair in your mouth."

The apartment was in a twelve unit apartment building on the corner of Franklin and Monument Avenue, in a historical residential part of the city filled with modest homes of middle class families, just a very short block from Monument Avenue's intersection with Sunken Road, where in 1862, hundreds of American men from the North and the South were killed, wounded or "missing in action," during the Civil War less than a hundred years before. As a teenager in the 1950s, I knew about that battle as did everyone who lived in that part of Virginia, but I wasn't thinking about any of that. I had my own civil war.

At once, I knew I wanted an after-school job. I had spent the last few years living in the country in a large old farmhouse, and the small apartment felt confining. Dad was living in DC, and Mom was still working at the cellophane factory where she had been working. Jan was in kindergarten. There wasn't much money floating around the family, and I didn't want to be home anyway. I made a plan to go downtown after school that afternoon. I went to my homeroom and the teacher assigned me a seat. Immediately, the boy behind me tapped me on the shoulder and said,

Hi, I'm Sam. Welcome."

When the bell rang for us to leave we stood up and talked for a moment while the other kids filed out. Sam went out ahead of me and started talking to an attractive girl standing next to the door, waiting to get in. I went on thinking, "Wow, is that his girlfriend?"

When I came home from school the first day, I walked downtown for my first-ever job-hunting expedition. I walked to Williams St, and started at the first business, Scottie's Bakery. No job. Next was a service station. Nope, nothing. Next, I walked up the hill, past the cemetery on Williams Street to a furniture store on the corner. No. Next door was a hardware and sporting goods store. Yes! The manager at Central Supply would hire me to sweep, dust and to serve customers when the regular clerk, Phyllis, was serving customers. I met Phyllis, and saw she was four or five years older than me I would be paid a dollar an hour, working two hours a day during the week, and from eight to five on Saturdays. I met Phyliss, who was four or five years older than me. I was happy for the first time in weeks. I had a real job that paid real money. in a nice, friendly place.

Central Supply was a small modern hardware store that sold lawn mowers, guns, ammunition, small hardware items, and sporting goods, including archery and fishing items. The manager usually stayed seated at his desk, which was half- hidden about six feet off of the floor in the back of the store, where he could watch and hear what was going on in the store. He seldom came down, but reigned over his kingdom from his personal castle, calling Phyllis or me back to stand below him as he gave instructions to us. A bell was screwed to the door at the top tinkled when the front door was opened I later learned that the store was owned by a very nice older man, Mr. Stoner, who also owned the big two-story hardware store in town, Fredericksburg Hardware, located a couple of blocks down Williams street, next to the local daily paper, the Free Lance-Star. Phyllis's husband, Jack, worked in the main hardware store.

The next day, Sam and I talked before the bell rang. As we walked oul he stopped to talk to the same girl again. I watched him do this every day for three or four days, and then one morning he was absent. As I left my homeroom I said to the girl,

"Sorry, Red, He's not here today."

Her face flushed, and I walked on, thinking how lucky Sam was. When he came in the next morning before the prayer and pledge of allegiance, I teased him about her.

"Hey, Sam, that's a good-looking girl you talk to every morning. I told her you weren't here yesterday."

"That's Michaela. We've been going steady for six months. She's a Junior."

"Well, she's good looking," I said.

Sam and I became friends, not really pals, but we were friends. Every day I watched him stop and talk to Michaela.

Neither Mom nor I ever had anyone visit in the apartment, because it was small, and packed with our furniture. Well, I did have three visitors once. One day in February the phone rang, and I answered it. It was Michaela, who lived five or six houses down Franklin Street from me.

"Since next week is Spring Break would you like to go on a double date to the movies with Sam and me Sunday night? My friend Ann who lives in Culpeper will be here and I thought you might want to go with us to the movies and see **Guys And Dolls**."

I happily agreed to go. I was excited.

Sunday came, and as planned, Dad picked me up early that morning for our day to work at the farm, remodeling the old house, which still had a lot of our belongings. Dad brought me back about four o'clock that evening and went on to DC. I took a shower and was getting ready for my date when the phone rang. It was the Mine Run Volunteer Fire Department, calling to tell us that the farmhouse was on fire, and they wanted Mother and Dad to come to the farm. Mother told me I would have to babysit my younger brother, ten-year old Jim, and five-year old sister, Jan. My friends could come over and watch TV, but I couldn't leave the apartment. I dialed Michaela's house and gave her the news. She said they would come over, and the date was still on. So much for never having anyone visit me in the apartment.

Dad picked up Mom and they left. The three kids came over, and the four of us talked about school, teased each other, and laughed at the funny things someone would say. I had the TV on with a very low volume, but we didn't really watch TV much, because Ann and I had to discover each other, and Sam and Michaela were getting better acquainted. Ann sat on the sofa, with Sam and Michaela. I sat in a chair next to Ann. Ann kept calling Michaela "Mickey," saying that's what she always called her. I liked Ann. She was smart, cute and had a great personality. In Orange, other than going to a couple of school dances without a date, and that one private party, I hadn't really been on a bonafide date, but I wasn't nervous, perhaps because Sam was my friend, and Ann and Michaela were so friendly. The two girls carried on a conversation that obviously had been going on for years, and I felt comfortable, but I was concerned about the farm, since the fire may be destroying all of my clothes I had left, including my FFA jacket that I hadn't brought, and my pictures, books, and the hundred things in high school that were the mementos and awards I had collected.

Mother and Dad got home later and said the house had burned completely. Nothing had been saved, so we lost all those things that we hadn't brought. which was a lot, because it served somewhat as a warehouse for our possessions. Every weekend Dad and I would get something, or put things back, depending on what we needed or wanted.

The following Sunday, we three children went down to

the farm with Mom and Dad. The bathtub that Dad and I had engineered to the second floor was lying on its side in the debris with the black cast iron showing where the white porcelain had melted. Pieces of the tin roof lay where the living room used to be. Only a few things were even able to be identified. It was positive proof that we would not be moving back to the farm any time soon, but Dad and I continued working there on Sundays, pulling out the debris, and burying it. It was 20 years before he rebuilt a home there, in a totally different part of the farm.

A month or so after we moved to Fredericksburg, I was walking down Kenmore on my way to school, past the apartments, when I spied a slender girl with a pony tail, in her wiggle skirt, who had turned the corner and was on Mary Ball Street just ahead of me. Looking again, I saw it was Peggy, a girl in my class.

"Peggy, Hold up," I called. She waited.

"Where do you live," I asked.

"In those apartments," she said as she pointed behind me where I had just passed.

"Neat. Do you mind if I walk with you?"

"No. I'd love it," she said as she moved her books around in her arms.

"Did you see Charlie Brown in the funnies this morning?" I asked.

She smiled. "Yes, Isn't Snoopy funny?"

"Yeah, He thought he had it made in the shade until the

cat clawed the roof off his house."

"Yes, did you see how the roof looked like the cat's paw went through it?"

"I know. That cat's a real 'cool cat'."

"Ha, ha. That's funny."

That almost exact conversation started us walking to school together for the rest of the year, with the opening conversation every morning about what Charlie Brown and Snoopy were up to. We only had a homeroom and one class together, and we became good friends, but since neither one of us were going on dates then, we never dated each other. Looking back, if I had asked her she probably would have accepted, but I didn't ask, and she never hinted. Both of us were too shy.

Michaela and one of her friends, Tomi, tap danced in the high school talent contest, and I saw her tap dance for the first time. It was the first time I had even seen a live tap dance. A couple of weeks later, while practicing tap dancing, she sprained her ankle and had to stay home for a couple of days, so I walked down the street to visit her one evening. She was camped out in a bed in a small den on the first floor, next to the living room where her parents were sitting. Michaela and I teased each other and talked for maybe an hour or so, and I left. It was just a neighborly visit, OK?

I had lived a screwed up life, and since this was my ninth new school, I was beginning to learn how to make friends in a hurry. This would be very helpful later in my life, allowing me to perform well in interviews and sell to people who didn't know me. My new friends here were what I would call an “elite, intellectual gang,” as all the members were smart seniors, with good grades. One boy was Emory, and was called “Big E,” by members of the gang and known as that by a lot of students. Big E was the only one of us who had a girlfriend, Elizabeth. Big E made top grades, was neat and “had it together.” He played the French horn and was in the band with me and “Dumb Owl,” which was the name for Al, who was the smartest of us all, especially in mathematics. Dumb Owl played the clarinet in the band. Two others in the gang, “Charlie Mac”, and “Big Dave” were not in the band.

A couple of other boys hung around but really weren’t considered in the “gang.” At lunch, George and Clyde (fake names) joined us. George was known for having green bean sandwiches for lunch. He claimed to like them. Sometimes I felt that “When God passed out brains, George thought he said ‘trains’ and let them go by,” a phrase that Dad often used on me and Jim. George’s grades were good, but it seemed that the simple things escaped him. Years later, at a ten-year class reunion, I heard that George had high-jacked a small one engine plane in Miami, and made the pilot fly him to Cuba where he was arrested, and supposedly was put in jail in Havana. I was shocked at first but then thinking about it, I wasn’t surprised. The whole thing would be typical of George.

Clyde was a wild man. As a senior, he was noted for dating an eighth-grade girl who most of us would have dated except the stigma of dating someone that young wouldn’t have been acceptable. The rumor was that he had been caught necking with her, and was slightly injured when her Dad threw Clyde out of the house in a scuffle. .

Sam was not a part of the group, nor was he in the band. Since my name was Richard, they named me "Big Dick," which everyone had fun with. That spring, Big E, Dumb Owl, and I played as a trio for the March of Dimes fundraiser downtown,when everyone laid a dime down on a long tape to cure polio. We sat on the back of a flatbed truck that was parked in front of Goolrick's Drug Store,

The gang, and Elizabeth, plus a couple other students were taking a class in trigonometry that I wasn't taking. The gang made up most of the class, which was one of the smallest classes in the school. Their teacher, Mr. Hosnick, ("Hoss" to the kids) lived in a house that I walked by every day to and from work. Often he was sitting out on the steps by the sidewalk, smoking a cigarette. Because he was a fun and friendly teacher, I would stop to chat, even though I didn't take any classes from him.

Knowing I was friends with his students, one day he said,

"Join us in trigonometry, It will be fun,"

The class was the same period as band class so I said,

"I only need the half credit from band class to graduate and if I flunk trig, I won't graduate."

"You won't flunk. I'll see to that."

This went on for a couple of days, when the band instructor who had heard from the gang that I didn't want to give up the band, told me that I could stay in the band and not come to practice, but I should go to trig. I really wasn't excited about dropping band class and taking trig, but I felt obligated, especially after "Hoss" told me I wouldn't fail, so I joined the gang in trig.

In my first test in trig, I had no idea how to solve the problems. My grade on the test was a gift at 15, probably because I had put my name on the paper. I panicked. Hoss said, "Don't worry about it. You'll be fine." In my second test I got a 60. I was still in panic mode. He reassured me with the same words again, "Don't worry about it. You'll be fine." I wasn't sure. At the end of the year, I was given a "D" and I graduated, but I never passed a test in trig.

As I'm thinking about those times walking to work, I remember I passed a couple of houses where black families lived. There was a boy about thirteen years old in his yard near the sidewalk, and when I saw him the first time we each said "Hi." The next time I saw him, I asked his name, and he replied, "Chris." I asked a question, he answered, and from that starting point, Chris and I deepened our conversations. We became friends in a town where such relationships were not acceptable, but I had been friends with Karen in an integrated neighborhood in DC, and I knew a personal relationship did not depend on race. Chris and I never talked beyond a few minutes on the days we saw each other, but I never forgot Chris. The memory of my friendships with Karen and Chris carried on and influenced my relationship with people of other races and cultures the rest of my life.

The money I was earning allowed me to buy Mom a candy bar every now and then, plus it provided me with the money to participate in school affairs. The Senior Class planned to go to New York City for two days toward the end of May for our graduation trip. I had saved my money, so I signed up along with the gang. Early one morning, about sixteen of the seventy Seniors boarded a chartered bus at the school, with two of our teachers as chaperones. We arrived in Manhattan in the afternoon. It was my first trip to the Big Apple, and I'm sure it was the first visit for most of the others as well.

That evening we went to dinner at Jack Dempsey's restaurant. Jack Dempsey had been the US Heavyweight Boxing Champion before he retired. I'll never forget when he came to our table, and I shook his hand, it seemed to be twice the size of mine, which really wasn't that small. Next, we went to Birdland, a famous nightclub then, and saw xylophonist, Lionel Hampton, perform. The club had an attractive "cigarette girl" in a revealing costume, with a tray held up flat in front of her by a strap around her neck. The tray had several brands of cigarettes that she was selling for a dollar a pack, an outrageous price because they were a quarter at any local drug store. Another woman in a sexy costume was taking people's photographs for a fee. None of us bought anything from either of them. At that time I didn't think it was unusual for me to be in a nightclub at age sixteen, along with fifteen other children, but I doubt that it would happen now. To my knowledge, none of us drank any alcohol, even though the drinking age at that time was eighteen.

If everyone in the group was eighteen or older maybe I was the only misfit. Maybe my being six feet tall helped me appear older. Maybe they just let anyone in if they paid the cover charge.

Later that night we went into the NBC studio to see the Tonight Show, starring Steve Allen, with Don Knotts, a genuine West Virginia guy. The show was telecast live then. Today it is taped in the late afternoon, and is broadcast later that night. This was before Jack Parr, and Johnny Carson who was the host for thirty years

After breakfast the next morning, we boarded the Grey Line Tour boat for a trip around Manhattan. The boat was almost full, and our group separated to get seats. After a few minutes, I got up to go see my friends in another part of the boat. As I walked down the aisle, I saw a very nicely-dressed girl, close to my age. As I passed, our eyes connected, and we each smiled. I said something and she responded. The tour conductor was on the loudspeakers rattling on about the UN Building, or something, and the motor was roaring, making it hard for us to hear each other, and since there was an empty seat beside her, I sat down.

She was an attractive eighteen-year-old high school senior, named Mary Jo, (fake name) on her senior trip from Greenbrier County, WV. (fake county). Since I was originally from Fayette County, WV, which was next to Greenbrier County, we immediately bonded. She introduced me to the girl sitting next to her, whose name I don't remember, and we talked about our lives. Then she said,

"I have a boyfriend, and...."

As she talked, I figured I was in his seat, and I immediately started looking around, so I could avoid a fight. On a boat. In Manhattan.

"Oh, I'm sorry!" I said, getting up to leave.

"It's OK. He joined the Army, and he's in Germany now." Relieved, my body relaxed. I sat back down.

"Just before he left, we got married." I tensed up again. As she talked, I relaxed.

The three of us talked for a few minutes, then she touched me and said,

"Why don't you walk with us back to the hotel after this ride is over?"

I looked at her friend. Her friend was smiling and nodding. I thought that would be fun, and increase the amount of time we would have together, and anyway, I wanted to see the New Yorker Hotel, (one of the finest in New York then), since they said they were staying there.

I went back to my group, but I didn't see the chaperones. I told one of the gang that I was going to walk a girl back to her hotel, and to tell the teachers that I would meet our group at the theater on Broadway where we were to see a matinee showing of ***Pajama Game*** at 2:30.

When the boat docked, Mary Jo, her friend, and I walked to the New Yorker, and went up to their room. As soon as the door closed, there was a pounding on the door. Mary Jo's friend opened it and their female chaperone burst into the room shouting at me:

"WHAT IN THE WORLD ARE YOU DOING IN HERE?? YOU HAVE NO BUSINESS BEING IN HERE!!"

I stuttered something and left in a hurry. I went back to our hotel and joined our group. I never really got to see what their room looked like, but I did see ***Pajama Game.***

The guys had spread the word that Big Dick had met a girl and would be back later. I told them it was over, but the rumors had spread, though the seniors, and afterward as it spread through the school, I caught a lot of teasing. I had made my impression on the students. I never heard any feedback from the teachers, but I'm guessing there were conversations about my behavior. I still wonder how Mary Jo's life turned out.

Mary Jo and I had exchanged addresses, and when I got home, I sent her a letter, but she never answered. I didn't mention the episode to my Mother, but I suppose she heard about it from the mother of Dumb Owl who she worked with. Months later, when I told Mother about the affair that wasn't, I said that I had never heard from Mary Jo. Mother snapped at me in that tough voice only mothers (mine anyway) have,

"Oh, she sent a letter. I tore it up."

She never told me what the letter said. I recognize the personal, emotional cloud she was living under at that time in her life, and I know now that her action was probably for the common good, especially mine. One never knows, but I've heard that forbidden fruit gives you a bad jam.

I wasn't the only bad character in Mom's life. My siblings get some credit for being at least a little bit bad. Even Jan had a part in it. Jan was in kindergarten. If she didn't have kindergarten she had a babysitter. Jan says more than once when she was outside playing with a friend she came inside to tell the babysitter that she wanted to show her friend her penny jar and she would take the jar outside, take out five pennies, bring the jar back inside and sneak across the street to the Mom and Pop store, and buy five pieces of penny candy. She says they were usually Tootsie Rolls and Mary Janes. Then she says she would share her treasure with her friend. Apparently it worked out OK until she tried it on Mom. Mom caught her red-handed and ended Jan's life she calls "petty crime."

Jim gets some blame for this story. On the way to and from work, I always walked by Michaela's house on Franklin Street. I was coming home from work one day, when she was out front. I stopped to say "Hi," when my brother Jim rode his bike up the street. He joined Michaela's and my conversation about Michaela's Jack Russell Terrier, Tinker, who was there with us. Jim suggested he give Tinker a ride in the basket that hung down next to the rear tire. I picked the dog up and put Tinker in the basket and Jim took off down the block. He came back just as Mrs. Miller came out of the house and saw Tinker in the basket. She gave Jim and me "very harsh words" for being careless with the dog as I took the uninjured Tinker out of the basket.

I never thought about it, but looking back, it seems Michaela was often sweeping the front porch and sidewalk about the time I was walking home from work, and, of course, I could never just pass without stopping to talk to her. I said something about the school band being in the parade on Decoration Day, (Memorial Day for the Yankees reading this). Michaela was a majorette in the band. I was surprised when she said,

"I'm not marching in the parade. I haven't practiced the new techniques, because of my ankle."

"Good. Then you can go with me and carry my trombone case," I teased.

"OK, I will," she said.

"Are you sure?" I asked.

"Yeah, it would be fun."

If she thought it would be fun, I was guessing she hadn't carried many trombone cases, because I never thought that was fun, but I was super excited that she said "yes," since as far as I knew, she was still dating Sam, and for her to be seen with me wouldn't be helpful in her relationship with him. Sure enough, on the day of the parade she walked with me to the parade's starting point and carried my case along the route of the parade, then we walked home together. The leaves were out in full force and waving at us from the trees, and the air was filled with that special spring scent that makes a spring day so special. I realized that being around someone you like makes the day special, too. It also causes a fluttering sensation inside.

Bill became a close friend of mine, even though he was not in the gang. Bill was a volunteer on the Rescue Squad, now called "First Responders." The Rescue Squad was next to the Sears store, and almost directly across the street from Central Supply where I worked. When a call came into the Rescue Squad, a horn on top of the building would honk three quick times in a row, for four or five times, to call in volunteers. I could hear the horn at home, inside the apartment with doors and windows closed. It was almost deafening being just across the street.

As a volunteer, Bill always had a gory story about an auto accident, farm equipment accident, or someone who was cut or shot. The Rescue Squad also delivered babies when needed. At that time, Bill assisted in the deliveries. Later, in 1959, when we reconnected, he had become a Virginia State Trooper and still volunteered on the Rescue Squad. By then, he said he personally had delivered over a hundred babies.

The school had a dress code. Long pants for the boys, and for the girls, skirts or dresses with appropriate lengths, and fully covered tops. Absolutely no slacks or pedal pushers. No one ever broke the rules, but Bill and I talked about it. Bill said,

"We ought to do something special for the last day of school."

My mischievous antenna went up.

"Yeah. What?"

Bill said, "I don't know, Let's think of something."

We fell silent for a minute then he said, "I know, let's wear Bermuda shorts."

I got on board his train of thought.

"Yes! I mean, they can't expel us for two weeks, it's the last day of school. It's graduation rehearsal day, anyway." I said.

Bill and I came to school the morning of the last day looking like we were dressed for the beach, even wearing sunglasses. The kids liked the concept. Mr. Sullins, the Principal, did not, and he intercepted us as soon as someone told him we were dressed inappropriately. He sent us home to change. We returned an hour later, properly dressed. Mr. Sullens, a wonderful Principal, did not impose any punishment.

As part of the Fourth of July Celebration, on Saturday night, the City Park Department sponsored a dance for teenagers at the playground at the lower end of Monument Ave. I still wasn't dating anyone, so I thought

I would just walk down to the park by myself to see who was there. Michaela was there dancing with Jack, (Fake name) a classmate of mine. As she danced with Jack, I broke in. When the music was over we talked for a minute, then Jack came back and asked for the next dance. She accepted. About halfway through the song, I broke in again. Jack gave up and went away, and Michaela and I danced the rest of the night together. I don't know what Jack did after he left us alone. I hope he found a nice girl, and I thank him for surrendering. After we danced the last dance, I walked Michaela home and kissed her good night under the porch light.

In my mind, that first kiss certified that I had a beautiful girlfriend.... I fluttered home from her house, full of fantastic feelings.

The next week, we went to the drive-in to see **Three Coins in the Fountain.** I have no idea what the movie was about. That summer, we would go to the movies, or she would put the top down in her Studebaker, and we would drive out to one of the Federal Parks where civil war fighting had occurred, have a picnic, and talk about our future. Sometimes we would cross the bridge and go to the Circle, a pizza and burger joint where we could dance to the jukebox. It was a summer of delight. Sometimes Summer said,

"Let's go get a frozen custard from Carl's." Yes, there was a Carl's frozen custard then. The outside seating wasn't there then, but the same delicious custard was. We had often stopped at Carl's five years before then, when we were going back to DC from working on the farm, when we first bought it. Carl's is old enough to be listed on the Register of National Historic Places. Heck, I'm old enough to be registered as a National Historic Customer.

When school had closed in June for the summer, I had performed well enough at Central Supply that Mr. Stoner, the owner of the two stores, expanded my hours to full time, and moved me to Fredericksburg Hardware's warehouse where the company had a pickup truck and a two-ton flatbed, for delivering items. I cut and threaded pipe, made plumbing nipples from short pieces of pipe, swept the floors, repaired lawn mowers, and delivered merchandise in the trucks. We sold plumbing supplies and roofing materials, plus bulky items. From working with Dad I already knew about everything plumbing, like the different types of 45 and 90 degree elbows, all sizes of nipples, and how to make them.

We also sold a lot of clothesline poles that we made from a piece of two inch diameter, eight-foot long, black pipe, with a four-foot cross piece welded on top. We had a welding company weld the crossbar on, and I drilled holes in the cross bars where the wire would be attached after the homeowner planted them in the ground. Then I painted the pipes with an aluminum-colored paint. I would deliver these poles to homes all over the county in the Ford two-ton flatbed, with a double-clutching two-stage, floor-mounted gear shift.

Oh, you don't know about double-clutching? I'm sure it's a lost art now, with automatic transmissions in big trucks. When you needed to change gears you put the clutch down and moved the gear shift to neutral. Then you let the clutch out, pushed it down again, and moved the gear shift into whatever gear you needed. On a double-clutching transmission if you don't do it just right, it won't go into gear. I learned quickly how to do it quickly. Ha! To deliver smaller items I used the 1948 Dodge five-window pickup truck that had two small windows in the rear corners of the cab, (making it a highly-regarded, rare, collectible pickup truck later) to deliver items as far away as the Marine Base in Quantico, up RT 1 toward DC.

Roland, the warehouse manager, and I were the only two people working in the warehouse. Roland taught me how to repair lawn mowers with Briggs and Stratton engines, and an occasional Kohler engine in the mix. Next to the office, against the wall in the warehouse was a flat-topped Pepsi cooler, always about half loaded where for a dime you could pull out a cold Pepsi or orange drink. But in the back row, thanks to Roland, you could pull out a plain-capped Pepsi bottle that had been refilled with moonshine. A couple of men would come in and pay Roland, put a dime in the cooler, and take out a bottle of "shine." I never knew how much you had to pay Roland to get a bottle.

Mr. Stoner was beginning to collect material for Stoner's Store, a museum he established in a house on Prince Edward Street that originally had been a part of Fredericksburg College in the 1700's. When he bought something large he would send me out in the pickup truck to bring it to the museum. The store has closed after years of service and has been dismantled. It is now a private home but it is fondly remembered by people who visited it.

1956 was a presidential election year, with the usual political conventions. In those days the conventions were broadcast on the radio during the day, since they were not striving for huge TV audiences as they are now. It was my first exposure to the national political stage, and I listened on the radio in the warehouse when I could. When I learned how the system worked, I developed an interest in politics. That interest never left me. The two candidates for president in 1956 were Eisenhower as the Republican candidate, and Adlia Stevenson running for the Democrats. Eisenhower eventually won his second term in November that year.

When Fredericksburg Hardware moved me to the warehouse full-time, I started work at 7AM. One morning as I walked by Michaela's house about 6:30, I heard her say "Hi" to me in a rather soft voice. I looked up and saw her looking at me from her upstairs bedroom window. We talked softly for a minute and I went on to work with a happy feeling. It started a habit that we followed every morning that summer as long as I lived on Monument Ave. She later told me that she set her alarm to wake up at 6:30, and after I walked by she would go back to bed and sleep until noon.

Just because the water is calm doesn't mean there aren't alligators in it.

I knew Mother wasn't really happy about my dating Michaela, because according to her, the Millers belonged to the Fredericksburg Country Club, and were part of Fredericksburg's "Society," but something set her off one day, and she blew up. In a loud voice, she shouted,

"YOU ARE TRYING TO FIT IN WHERE YOU SHOULDN'T! THEY ARE "FFV's!" (First Families of Virginia.)

"YOU KNOW WHAT THAT MEANS DON'T YOU??

"No."

"THAT MEANS THEIR S**T DOESN'T STINK!!" she exploded.

I kept my mouth shut.

Never mind that the Millers were from Colorado, not Virginia, and Michaela's father taught accounting and shorthand at Mary Washington College, (an all girls' college at that time,) and worked part time as an outside bookkeeper/accountant for three or four small businesses in town, and my father was an attorney.

Three of the boys in our "intellectual gang" were from wealthy families and did live in expensive houses. Charlie Mac's family gave him an almost-new Ford that Charlie used when he hauled our gang around if we went out at night. Michaela's parents weren't wealthy, but I had met several of the Millers' friends, and, yes, some were enormously wealthy, from family farms that had been passed down for generations, and some owned successful businesses, and they all belonged to the Fredericksburg Country Club, but almost all of them were friendly, down-to-earth people.

With some coaching from Michaela, and her mother, I had learned how to recognize all the various silverware only used at formal dinners, for example, I knew an oyster fork when I saw one. I knew how to eat with asparagus tongs, and the proper use of three or four different table knives, and various upper class customs. Mother and Dad had taught us the basic tools of etiquette and manners, but what I learned from Michaela and her "FFV" parents would enable me later to confidently go to formal events and meals dressed in formal wear in the Plaza Hotel in New York City, the Mayflower in DC, or any formal dinner, with an ability to function properly without anxiety, or self-doubt. Dad had a habit of questioning Jim and me while playing courtroom with us at the dinner table, and through the years Jim and I had learned the original **Roberts' Rules of Order,** plus Dad's own personal

"Jennings Roberts' Rules of Order," and how to use our minds in an analytical manner.

So from our parents we learned how to function in the legal and practical world, and that later helped me immensely in places like managing and participating in trade associations, serving on state legislative committees, and lobbying in the halls of the state legislatures. In all types of meetings and circumstances I had much more confidence since I had been exposed to those basics. It was all a part of my learning.

My mother was having to deal with the same situation that her mother dealt with years ago, when my mother grew out of the social circle where she was born.The difference was, I wasn't going to leave her with a child to raise. I would eat in the Mayflower in DC, where she had worked, and the Plaza in New York, owned by the first Mrs. Donald J. Trump. I would own a tuxedo. I would advise legislators and governors, I would fly on private jets, and travel the US, Canada, and Mexico. I would be a country club member, play golf at country clubs in several states, in two countries, and eat escargot drenched in garlic.

I'm not sure how Fred and Rene Miller felt about me, this 6 ft. 2 inch tall, 165 lb. skinny kid, with unruly hair, who was dating their daughter, but they were always pleasant, (unless I was putting the dog in Jim's bicycle basket), and seemed to always be supportive of Michaela. One of Mr. Miller's (Fred) part-time jobs was being the accountant (he was not a CPA) for the Richmond, Fredericksburg, and Potomac Railroad, (RF&P) an old railroad company that had been founded in the 1840's. The RF&P had been a pawn in the civil war. The Yankees used it to move troops into the South. By the 1950s the RF&P only owned some tracks between Richmond and Fredericksburg that the other train lines ran on. Now there was no equipment, but the RF&P "rented" their track to every railroad company that ran on their tracks. All of RF&P's income came from the "tolls" that the other railroads paid to the R.F.&P whenever a train ran over their tracks. Fred told me the locals said the abbreviation, R.F.&P. stood for Run Fast, & Push.

When he found out about my interest in broadcasting, Fred took me down to see one of his other accounts, WFVA, the local radio station. At six o'clock every evening during the week, after the six o'clock news, the station had a young DJ who played popular music, which I liked, and listened to when I got home from work. One evening I heard him say:

"I'm going to play some old, some new, and some "Born To Be With You."

That's a song sung by the Chordettes, who sang "Mr. Sandman." I liked the song "Born To Be With You", but apparently not as much as the DJ. Without talking, he played the song on the air for forty-five minutes. It was his last broadcast from WFVA.

My grades weren't great, so my guidance counselor, Mrs Chick, recommended that I apply to the University of Richmond, and skip applying to Harvard. Michaela was just starting her senior year at James Monroe. I would only be fifty miles away, and I figured some of the boys at Richmond would be dating Mary Washington girls, so occasionally I could catch a ride to Fredericksburg to see her.

I didn't know it then, but the University of Richmond

was the college where John-Boy of the Waltons went. Actually, the TV show, The Waltons, was based around a book, **Spencer's Mountain**, written by Earl Hanmer, Jr, about his family that lived in the mountains near Charlottesville (not far from Orange). Earl Hamner, Jr. was the original John-Boy. The book was made into a movie titled **Spencer's Mountain** in which Hollywood put the location in Wyoming. In the book, Clay-Boy, (name change), went to the U of Richmond, as Earl Hamner, Jr actually did before I did. Later when I worked at WRVA-TV, one of the engineers I worked with was the son of one of the Walton boys, and so, was the nephew of Earl Hamner, Jr. I only applied to the University of Richmond, and I was accepted by them. I was going to live in the city that I had seen pasted on the front of those Greyhound buses years ago, and only imagined living there.

Meanwhile, Dad was doing well in his profession as the attorney for the Washington National Airport, and In mid-August Mother and Dad reunited in Alexandra in a rented row house. Since I was still working at the hardware store, I had a couple of weeks I could work, and because I needed the money, I moved north with the family to Alexandria, and slept in the basement, getting up each morning to walk a couple of blocks to Rt 1 to catch a 5:30 AM Greyhound to Fredericksburg, and return home on an afternoon bus.

Thankfully that was only two weeks, so in late August 1956, I loaded my few possessions in Dad's '55 turquoise Plymouth. No need for a truck, or things packed in the back seat. A suitcase full of clothes and a small box of possessions in the trunk of the car was all there was. No radio, no calculator (There were no hand-held calculators until the late '70's.) no trombone. Mother and Dad took me to the University of Richmond. After we got directions as to where my room was located, Dad stopped in front of one of the ugly, narrow, two-story green wooden barracks that had been built on campus during WWII for the U.S. Army.

I took my suitcase and box of possessions out of the car, and Mother and Dad immediately left, honoring an unspoken agreement between us. It had been an exciting eight months in Fredericksburg, and a screwed-up six years with my parents, but at sixteen, I was free. The hard places in life had made me stronger. All of that screwed-up life hadn't killed me. I was stronger. I would be fine this time. I carried my suitcase up the steps to my next new life.

ABOUT THE AUTHOR Ri**chard A. Roberts** is a memoir author and storyteller who brings 20th-century American life vividly to the page. His journey as a writer began in sixth grade with a school report on Olympic figure skater Sonja Henie—an early sign of the lifelong love for writing that would shape his future. Born in West Virginia, Richard's early experiences in one-room schoolhouses during the 1940s gave him a front-row seat to a way of life few remember today.

With decades of real-world experience and a passion for preserving forgotten stories, Richard writes compelling nonfiction books filled with historical insight, humor, and heartfelt memories. His books are especially popular with readers who enjoy stories about growing up in mid-century America, the Appalachian experience, and reflections on how the country has changed since the 1940s and 1950s.

He has lived in West Virginia, Virginia, Pennsylvania, Maryland, Ohio, Illinois, and South Carolina. These life experiences—paired with a sharp memory and a storyteller's voice—bring his writing to life in a relatable, engaging way. Richard is a proud father, grandfather, and great-grandfather. Through two marriages, he has seven children, twenty grandchildren and twenty great-grandchildren. He often jokes that with a family this big, his family may just take over America by 2060.

Follow Richard's journey at: writerrichardroberts.com and explore his books about stories of America.

Ri**chard A. Roberts** is a memoir author and storyteller who brings 20th-century American life vividly to the page. His journey as a writer began in sixth grade with a school report on Olympic figure skater Sonja Henie—an early sign of the lifelong love for writing that would shape his future. Born in West Virginia, Richard's early experiences in a one-room schoolhouse during the 1940s gave him a front-row seat to a way of life few remember today.

His personal memoirs explore growing up in rural Appalachia, the shift from country life to city living in Washington, D.C. and Virginia, and the cultural changes that shaped postwar America.With decades of real-world experience and a passion for preserving forgotten stories, Richard writes compelling nonfiction books filled with historical insight, humor, and heartfelt memories. His books are especially popular with readers who enjoy stories about growing up in mid-century America, the Appalachian experience, and reflections on how the country has changed since the 1940s and 1950s.

He has lived in West Virginia, Virginia, Pennsylvania, Maryland, Ohio, Illinois, and South Carolina. These life experiences—paired with a sharp memory and a storyteller's voice—bring his writing to life in a relatable manner.

His personal memoirs explore growing up in rural Appalachia, the shift from country life in West Virginia to city living in Washington, D.C. and Virginia, and the cultural changes that shaped postwar America. A graduate of Virginia Commonwealth University, Richard worked his way through college while raising a family—an experience that gave him valuable insight into the human stories behind everyday life.

Richard A. Roberts is a memoir author and storyteller who brings 20th-century American life vividly to the page. His journey as a writer began in sixth grade with a school report on Olympic figure skater Sonja Henie—an early sign of the lifelong love for writing that would shape his future. Born in Fayette County, West Virginia, Richard's early experiences in a one-room schoolhouse during the 1940s gave him a front-row seat to a way of life few remember today. His personal memoirs explore growing up in rural Appalachia, the shift from country life to city living in Washington, D.C. and Virginia, and the cultural changes that shaped postwar America. A graduate of Virginia Commonwealth University with a business degree, Richard worked his way through college while raising a family—an experience that gave him valuable insight into American business, hard work, and the human stories behind everyday life.

With decades of real-world experience and a passion for preserving forgotten stories, Richard writes compelling nonfiction books filled with historical insight, humor, and heartfelt memories. His books are especially popular with readers who enjoy stories about growing up in mid-century America, the Appalachian experience, and reflections on how the country has changed since the 1940s and 1950s.

He has lived in West Virginia, Virginia, Pennsylvania, Maryland, Ohio, Illinois, and South Carolina, and has traveled through 47 U.S. states, Canada, and Mexico. These life experiences—paired with a sharp memory and a storyteller's voice—bring his writing to life in a relatable, engaging way.